BASIC IDEAS OF

National Socialist
Cultural Policy

Wolfgang Schulz

Published by Invisible Empire Publishing LLC © 2026

Hardcover ISBN: 978-1-963591-12-5

Original Published Year 2023
New Edition Published Year 2026

Printed in the United States of America

INVISIBLE EMPIRE
PUBLISHING

Trigger/Offensive Content Warning and General Disclaimer:

From the extensive literary remains of our unfortunately much too soon departed party comrade and editor.

– Dr. Wolfgang Schulz

We publish as the first this work of the deceased devoted to National Socialist cultural policy. Berlin, in March 1939.

– Dr. Matthias Ziegler - Reich Office Leader in the office of the Führer's deputy for the whole spiritual and worldview education of the NSDAP.

CONTENTS

CONTENTS

PUBISHERS FORWARD

Basic Ideas of Nationalist Socialist Cultural Policy is translated from the Third Reich original Grundgedanken nationalsozialistischer Kulturpolitik by Munich university professor Wolfgang Schulz, which was published by the central publishing house of the NSDAP (Franz Eher Verlag) in 1939 after the authors death.

The objective of this policy was to promote a culture that remained true to folk and race and hence promoted the spiritual, biological health, and integrity of both. The original translation has been reviewed, corrected, and altered for better clarity and readability for the 21st century reader.

ORIGINAL FORWARD

This book turns to the service duty and service readiness of the worker and of the political soldier in the spiritual as well and calls him to deal with the facts and ideas presented here, to ponder them and imprint them upon himself, in order to develop them further in both directions: to his own image of our culture, as it must be so that we can survive, and to his energy to give this image, wherever he can, combative consequence and effect.

An introduction of such kind was previously lacking. It wants to provide the basic knowledge for application in the daily struggle; it wants to be an instruction book and simultaneously learning book, but in the new sense, not static, rather dynamically, not resting within itself, rather moved by inner forces, not merely portrayal of an object, which - because of its inexhaustibility and because we must first conquer it for ourselves in many parts - cannot conclusively portrayed, rather already plan and guideline for this campaign for the conquest of a totality, where nothing less is at stake than our German future.

The most marked, concise language and portrayal manner, emphasized at the decisive places, want to accommodate this inner claim and the outer form, for which we have the publishing house to thank good paper, large, clear typography and enough margin for one to make notes.

This book does not present any prerequisites regarding the reader's previous education, but with the one minor exception: race science and the science of heredity and their application to the German folk, hence the basic features of National Socialist population policy, must presumed to be present, leastwise in their basic features, because of the wealth of publications about this topic and the previous schooling work.

But the application of general life-science and life-causal (biological) knowledge to the cultural formation of the races and folks in important details and even in main issues has not yet sufficiently thought through and intelligibly portrayed. Many obscurities, misunderstandings and insecurities were the result.

In order to counter that, in the first part about *"Heredity and Culture"*, I have distinguished between the genes, the traits growing from these genes as racial properties of the first order and the cultural and legacy values as racial properties of the higher order (the separation into racial properties of first and higher order is not to be taken in the sense of a valuation, rather of a counting - the publisher) and pointed out the rooting of all value in the primal behavior of the living. Through, I could make the cultural process visible as transmutable and elevated repetition of the hereditary processes, point out the dangers that lie and have previously led to the decline of the high cultures, and show the nature-given paths to banish these dangers.

In this first part, at the end of the second portion, the world-view decisive practical applications result at the conclusion of the *"World Historical and Intellectual Historical Review"* of the struggle of the Nordic racial soul for meaning in the world.

The Nordic folks founded their five high cultures outside their ancestral region and amidst already beginning race-mixing. The objection that high culture thus rests on race-mixing only falls when one has understood the life-science and life-causal (biological) side of the world-historical process. It is developed here for the first time in its essentials.

The Nordic folks have, one after the other down to their last great reserve, down to us Germans, despite all their glorious deeds ultimately failed world-historically. The confidence that we will not likewise fail, rather reach the goal, if we just want to and remain strong in our unshakeable faith, likewise receives its full support only through life-causal insights. Hence, I have at the conclusion of the 'World-Historical and Intellectual-Historical Review", again confronted the dangers of failure, which lie in the racial properties of higher order, with the monumental task.

The emphasis lies in the *"World-Historical and Idea-Historical Review"*, thus in the second part. Worldview preconditions, if this expression is supposed to have meaning, a view of the world, at least in its elements, is decisive for our existence. We cannot satisfy ourselves with a rigid picture of the world as it is at the present. Rather, we must penetrate to the working, moving forces, which rise in the far removed past and push into the most distant future. The most important of these forces in the river of blood. It is our cause that is at stake in world history.

Hence, we begin the review of the world with the homeland.

I see nowhere in the publications about homeland science, homeland instruction, homeland and folk that one has already taken the race ideal seriously and finally given to the homeland concept, derived from the Nordic, new content, which is deepened, guiding and guaranteeing political will formation. If one also gives the benefit of prehistory, German ethnology science and much else to homeland instruction, that still does not take effective action, if blood is not recognized as the shape of the soil and the homeland of the blood is understood as the genuine homeland. Without that, homeland stupor threatens to again and again lend a hand to the penetration of all liberal-democratic clerical-political narrow-hearted or even separatist and camouflaged political-denominational tendencies.

Only the homeland concept grasped deeply by the Nordic race and the love of homeland purified by it as love (Minne), that means as a loving memory of our prehistory, it is again immediately about the whole of our National Socialist cultural-political action.

The great processes through which the Nordic race, hence our blood, under its inner content triumphed in the cultural history of humanity, was previously not recognize at all, or one presented it only poorly and distorted. I have tried to depict it fully and in the right conditions.

A world history on racial foundation, which would suffice for the justified claims, has yet to be created. But even it was to already exist, it would be necessary to solidify its result, so that it can be absorbed, surveyed and noted without too many details, in order, as force-driven overall picture, to determine further thought and behavior in terms of worldview (and not as bloodless concepts).

If this segment is imprinted, one can in later repetition still also fill it with wealthier content. One will find catchwords for it everywhere, and books that can help are listed at the conclusion. The danger of losing oneself will hardly still threaten if the guiding summary of meaning has overall already become intellectual property.

The cultural deeds of the Nordic folks are presented in the third chapter in their intellectual result according to the branches of science and of *"German education"*. Each subject receives its direction toward a whole, which is sketched in terms of worldview, not subjectively. It is rooted on a view that is based on world-history and cultural history, which pushes from the past into the future and does not follow personal views, guesses and wishes, rather takes as guideline blood-tied, supra-personal knowledge and desire.

The subjects are evaluated according to their life-causal significance. Here as well, a correctly gained overall view must be inwardly possessed, so each can see what matters chiefly to him from the standpoint of the connection, and each guide himself accordingly. Training and education determine, to a very large degree, the future countenance of the nation and must make sure that it does not perish.

The discussion of the preparing and accompanying questions surrounds this three-part core; a listing of books and publications that can be brought in later is added.

Our path as folk and race is merely the end of an incomparably longer and much broader path of fate; for the path of our race and of the other world-historically significant races would have to be integrated into the history of the whole of humankind, this into the development of living beings overall, so then life into the overwhelmingly great framework of non-living nature. Finally, all that would have to be confronted by the spirit of the human being of Nordic race in his overall performance spanning this entire world, his bearing, his strength of will. Only that would produce worldview overall.

But the part that is at stake here, as contradictory as this may seem, is more than the whole. For this whole of our comprehensible world, picture itself depends on the existence of this part: without the Nordic race, without the German folk, without us - there is no such world recognition and hence also no action directed accordingly.

Hence, this time we limit ourselves to empathize from the whole the world-view foundations which are necessary, namely for our existence and our National Socialist cultural policy, which must secure this existence.

One should proceed from what the daily press brings under the caption *"cultural policy"*. But one should not stop with theatre, film, entertainment, art and science and the daily struggle for these and all other cultural accomplishments. Instead, one should penetrate to the fundamental. It lies in that, first, we must push back everything foreign that wants to crowd out and falsify our cultural values, second, that we come to ourselves and must reach the essential, third, that we must take the path to that mode that bears everything. What mode that is, is taught overall, and hence compellingly only, by world history and the history of ideas, and what significance is inherent in the just presented trinity is taught in the chapter *"Heredity and Culture"*.

What is present here is the extensively expanded and extensively reworked edition of a submission that has already been published in 1934 under the title *"The Racial and Folkish Basic Idea of National Socialism"* in the collected works *"The Administration Academy, A Handbook for the Official in the National Socialist State"* (Industrieverlag Spaeth & Linde, Berlin). The book edition now makes it available to the public, even for schooling as well.

The intention to serve schooling imposed upon me the greatest reserve in the expounding of personal views. But it was also not to be avoided, since the object must first be worked out and its picture is not complete by a long shot. Also, I harbor the conviction that only personality can school, and hence, everywhere I have something personal to offer, I also step forward with it decisively. It will be easy for the attentive user to discern this at many places and especially overall. It is about philosophical - I want to say: worldview -, religious, artistic, political convictions, and these, as Alfred Rosenberg has rightly stressed - are to be seriously founded only under the precondition of personal freedom of conscience. Neither the movement nor the user of the book can and should be tied down by them. But what I give here should indeed offer organized documents and stimuli for formation of judgment. And precisely that is the purpose of all genuine schooling.

This book has not been written according to other books, rather from the whole, not for the eyes, which hastily glide over the lines, rather for the ears that listen, and aside from that with the unconditional will to serve the rejuvenation of our folk from its life-causal and world- historical conditions under the sign of National Socialism.

The bearing is a fighting one, the goal reflection. Between the battles lies the resting position, the preparation, the planning, the securing, the watch. The warrior on lonely watch is all the more intimately bound to his community. The more his pondering stretches, the deeper it flows from the soul.

The moments of inner contemplation give clarity, firmness, strength. Because this book wants to awaken contemplation, give firmness, donate strength, it is dedicated to the dead of the war, the dead of the movement, eternal Germany!

Munich, in summer 1936.

Wolfgang Schultz.

CHAPTER

1

INTRODUCTION

National Socialist politics, and hence the part of it that one can designate cultural policy, is determined, and carried out by the Führer and those summoned by him for the individual tasks.

If one wants to know what National Socialist cultural policy is, then one should look at these men, at what they do, and to the guidelines that they give to draw along responsible co-workers, and at the legislation that paves the way for this work.

What plays out there, history will one day characterize and evaluate. And one will then be able to write above a portion of the history of National Socialism: National Socialist cultural policy.

The unity of action is guaranteed by the unity and organized gradation of the leadership, by the party program and the publications of the movement, by the common experience of the period of struggle and by the National Socialist worldview. Its two basic ideas are race and folk.

Race & Folk

National Socialism does not aim unconditionally at bringing new ideas, and the ideas of race and folk as well are certainly not new. But it wants to restore the nation's previously despised values and does this from a depth of desire and from a totality claim that is new.

Through the movement that the Führer has called to life and carried ever farther forward, prerequisites exist such as never existed, and power is also at disposal to achieve the necessary. So, the overall picture is totally different, and through this the old ideas as well gain new coloration and signification.

We do not proceed from speculations about the community, about a theoretical universalism and about the contrast to the general concept of the individual in order to deduce from its National Socialism, rather from our own present-day, historical, racial, life-causal conditioned folk community itself. This orientation is socialist down to the bone and even into its marrow. It demands that this community guides itself according to the forces that determine its existence and, if they are correctly used, secure, purify and elevate it. Employment of all means of the folk community in the service to its task - that is socialism.

A folk does not propagate itself through the race idea alone, through knowledge of the value of its blood alone, and not through the resultant rebellion of thought, rather only through the mastering of all of its life conditions, even the economic. The share of the folk comrades in this mastering, their performance, is diverse, just as they themselves are diverse, and maximum manifold value is determined and developed accordingly. The goal and the means that are suitable to make it achievable for the folk comrades, hence our socialism, is among us Germans something quite different from in any other folk. We are simply not socialists, rather National Socialists.

Everything that we have is employed. The unshakeable faith in the great goal lays the foundation, a new way of thinking grows out of it. It is not nourished solely by this faith, rather also purified by all attainable knowledge coming into question for its execution, which must be made ready for this purpose, thought through anew and conscientiously checked for its applicability, the less important recedes and the essential in the service of the new overall task stands out. The spiritual goods of the nation experience a total mobilization and get inner direction and unity. The racial and folkish idea stands at the focal point, such as corresponds to its fundamental importance.

The Old Demand

How deeply this idea is rooted in German history is illustrated by two names: Ernst Moritz Arndt and Friedrich Ludwig Jahn.

Arndt was the first who, with his little noticed *"Attempt at a Comparative History of the Folks"*, rolled out the history of the European folks as blood picture. Ludwig Scheman, the renowned researcher of the history of the race idea, passes this verdict against him: *"With all enthusiasm, more Nordic prudent than Gobineau and with all prudence more soaring than Woltmann, he was already expected both in the basic doctrines."*

At Arndt's side stands Jahn, who was the first to coin the concept and term nationality (Volkstum), present race as core essence and pronounce the three great demands: racial purity, folk unity, freedom of thought. This trinity is pure, correct and leading; for half-breeds with their conflicted souls bring conflict and prevent any unity of the folk; the spirit remains constrained, foreign powers put it under their spell.

Freedom here is not liberalism, rather the fulfilment of one's own inner law. The care of the race secures the unity of the folk and liberates its genuine, culture-bearing spirit.

The New Realizations

Since Arndt and Jahn, nothing fundamental had changed in the demand, but much and fundamental has changed in the purification and deepening of the ideas. Today it is also no longer about a mere demand, rather we stand in the middle of fulfilling it.

The connection between the races, the nationalities and the cultures of the folks was researched down to many details.

Comparative linguistics has outlined and presented the Indo-Germanic branch of folks, and comparative anthropology has done the same for the Nordic race. It has been shown that the bearing stratum of Indo-Germanic man and the Nordic race are the same. The most important cultures of world history have become tangible as expression of the northern racial essence. Research of artefacts has further enriched and deepened these realizations.

The spiritual legacy of Germanic and Indo-Germanic antiquity has proven itself as unexpectedly plentiful and valuable treasure. From Indo-Germanic man to Germanic man, a clearly discernible line of physical descent and spiritual-moral unity runs to our German present and points into our future.

The composition of the German folk, of its tribes and professions from elements of various highly valuable races and the leading importance of the Nordic racial core, which is most firmly preserved in the peasantry, clearly stands before us. The distribution of hereditary traits in the populace is open to our view. Several important laws of heredity have been discovered.

All these results demand that they now finally be used, and it is self- evident that in a time in which the distress of the folk, but also its self- awareness and its awakened energy, demand final action, we will also really employ them with conscientious determination.

Fourfold Cultural Policy Verification Test

We must prove ourselves to four significant witnesses: first, to our history, second, to our folk, third, to its culture, and fourth, to the folks and cultures around us.

We see before us German history, full of glorious achievement, but also burdened with many grave failures.

One should think about the words that Ulrich von Hutten spoke in 1818 in his speech about the war with the Turks: *"There lives in Germany a sturdy youth, big hearts greedy for genuine glory, but the guide, the leader, is missing. So that energy dies, valor slackens, glowing thirst for deeds decays in the darkness."*

Today, we have the leader. The old parties have been destroyed, the provinces, tribes and professions are united, and things are achievable that recently still seemed impossible.

We see before us the German folk full of incomparable talent, but also burdened with many defects.

Our population policy must remove the defects, secure the procreation of the congenitally healthy and restrain the proliferation of the congenitally ill. Our race policy must support the bearing race of our nationality, whereas one previously despoiled it, yes, raged against it. We can solve both tasks; for we have the realizations of genetics, the admittance of the existence of the genes and the racial elements of the populace and the insight into the leading importance of the Nordic race.

We see before us German culture, which is splendidly plentiful in its scope and can compare itself with the cultures of all the surrounding folks, if it does not even surpass them in many things.

But this culture as property does not yet satisfy us. We must not merely preserve what has been achieved and secure it against decay; we must not just administer a past. The new ideas and the new will of our present obligate us to view our past and the opportunities of our future with fresh eyes, to learn from this and to act accordingly. We see in our culture many impurities, many tears, and fissures, much foreign that was imposed upon us and contradicts our nature, does not let us find ourselves and rarely lets us be fully happy.

So next to the comforting awareness of our old inherited and mighty culture as possession steps, the rousing demand: culture as a goal. Expulsion of the foreign growth from the native - a long-term work, but simultaneously a task that finally gives us a future again.

The culture-creative significance of the Nordic race, which has presented itself in the Indo-Germanic cultures of antiquity, in Germanic culture and in the German cultural process, is the world-historical proof that we must nurture the core element of this race in the German folk and base the spiritual goods of the German future upon it.

Finally, we look at the folks and cultures around us and are aware of much respect and love, but also deepest hatred, which surrounds us and threatened our existence especially seriously, when we were still defenseless. That is past, but we need friends especially now.

The healthier we are as folk body, the more confident as bearer of a uniform culture, the more we will justify and find friendship.

The Nordic race, upon which our culture must build, does not need to display the so-called Nordic reserve. Rather, it can and should also bridge over. The more thoroughly we explore, the more clearly we see ourselves tied to the surrounding folks in a great cultural community from olden times, which owe their best in their own native manner to the same racial foundation.

Just as National Socialism is the great bulwark of Europe and of the White race overall against Bolshevik chaos, so is the racial and folkish idea of National Socialism the surest guarantee of peace and agreement among the folks and simultaneously the guarantee to preserve the cultural values of its old civilizations.

History & Politics

The doubts against the use of the racial and folkish ideas of National Socialism and against the warriordom (Kämpfertum), the *"activism"*, which lies within them, are as old and baseless as the world that this combativeness has already swept away. The representatives of that overly clever world and we - how do we stand toward each other?

We champion the primacy of political will over the historic process; they claim that the historical process invariably continues its own without this and also forms the will. We likewise believe the latter, only with us it has a different meaning. We only shout that a will, which revolts and with heroic determination reaches for the impossible - makes not only it possible, rather achieves it.

We believe that from the realization of such come new drives of the will that overcome the supposed necessities, and we use our freedom, which lies; they teach everything obeys necessity and that it does not help to rebel against it. But they deny simultaneously the possibility of all politics, such as their own as well, has turned out correspondingly poorly.

History is supposed to be a wheel that rolls across us, and it is decried as lunacy to want to grab into the spokes. Just, what does history, a life process, into which the decisions of the will of distinguished men intervene again and again, have in common with a lifeless wheel?

Or should history progress through thesis and anti-thesis to higher union (synthesis) or higher level of culture according to an inherent (*"dialectic"*) logic, and should the future be decided by this and not by answers, found in time or fatefully neglected, to favorable or threatening reality? To a weak, over-stimulated thinking, the sequence of cultural levels seemed so much like something changing and escalating because of necessary impulses that culture was supposed to be the same thing as a structured, independent being that comes over man; he has its booty while he is its creator, and it is weak if he tries.

Even Goethe thought the same thing, that the necessary constantly repeated itself on a higher level, in the image of a spiral. But what with him was a brilliant equation, tempted an immense throng of sophists to get on the track of such escalating orbits and to force the numbers of world history into simplistic formulas, yes, to want to predict the future from them. Just, the plough must not be invented, because the 500 years of whatever theory are over, rather because a peasant folk already exists as a seed that wants it. History is instructive like life, but mostly because it never repeats itself exactly, and because each historical situation is unique occurring once, which awaits its master who overpowers it.

Folk Convalescence

It is a welcomed objection that one still does not know all the laws, that the final insight has not yet been achieved, and that hence one must not yet apply what one already knows. One raises this objection, especially gladly against genetics and its applications in race policy and population policy.

But research is never at an end, rather must always continue. In all other branches of science, it is so, even in the so-called exact ones of mathematics, physics and chemistry. Technology has never failed to use also, immediately applying the scientific knowledge and laws that one had gained.

Experience and growth of scientific knowledge later expands and simplifies such applications, but both would never come about if one wanted to wait for a terminal condition of completed insight, which is eternally denied to limited human intellect because of the infinity of nature.

Hence, we must also use the knowledge of genetics that we already have without prejudice to future knowledge that will hopefully come later. A congenitally healthy breed, which we can already bring about with the already known means, will also harvest such fruits sooner, and it will certainly more easily accomplish much that we achieve only with effort. The beginning is the hardest; it is more necessary. But precisely that terrifies those whose advantages lie in the old damages.

The false doctrine that all human beings are the equal still haunts heads and resists the fundamental truth of the inequality of human beings according to their appearance, their genes, and their accomplishments. The valuation of human beings that results from this is portrayed as arrogance of the more valuable, yes, as injustice.

One scorn our desire as racial arrogance, without noting that we do not judge the individual according to race, rather according to accomplishment. But regarding the folk whole, we are concerned about the race, because the Nordic race alone has over the course world history passed a performance test that is so mighty that it obligates us to also employ this race for the new, even far greater accomplishments that matter now.

The old cultures, and at their top the cultures of the Indo-Germanic folks, have achieved the mightiest things, but not the final one, the securing of their own existence. They have perished. Inner dangers threaten our culture and by external ones. Will we reach our goal? Will we secure the survival of our culture, and will we be able to increase it and pass it on, elevated, to the future of our folk? If we fail, we who are basically the last large remnant of the Nordic race, then the civilization of our race, yes, of humankind, is for centuries and millennia in danger and probably lost. If we succeed, then we are saved.

It is a world historical moment without equal that we must face, and it is our will to make ourselves fit to pass it.

Culture as Goal

For those who view culture simply as possession, that is incomprehensible. For them, German nationality is a pillow upon which they want to fall asleep in laurels, while for us it is a task that places the hardest demands but is also full of promises.

We want to take our nationality under care, to keep it away from harmful influences. One mocks that as prudery; the charm of culture supposedly lies only in diversity of touches. Well, we are fed up with this over-stimulation and will abolish it.

Or one says: Culture must grow, one cannot manufacture it artificially. Just what previously proliferated among us were the weeds, and we want to exterminate them so that the beautiful and noble plants, which until now often withered or even died, can better thrive.

Cultures need their care like forest, field, and garden, and indeed a reasonable one that accounts for the laws of nature and increases them to greater beauty and order.

Forester, farmer, and gardener must love nature, must understand it intimately, but must also know and have learned much about it so that the growth entrusted to them does to grow wild or become desolate.

In municipal constructions, land planning and monument maintenance, the technical and historical knowledge comes in as well. In the trades, production, trade, even more so in schooling and education system of a folk, in art and science, the tasks reach down to the last demands of the moral and spiritual.

All that only grows correctly if it is nurtured. And the same thing as for every one of these and for many other cultural tasks of a folk is also true for culture overall and for all cultural policy.

Love for a folk and insight into it and the realities of the land and its resources are the foundations, and all indifference that makes the excuse that *"nothing is to be done"* is totally alien to us. Usually, it is just pretended and the cloak behind which all kinds of groups and cliques pursue their own selfish goals, often unabashedly.

Or one says we have no sense for the historical realities and completed facts. And yet, we derive precisely from the historical reality the proof of the value of race and nationality. Certainly, we do not recognize completed facts. Rather, if we are Germans, we will not tire to push for the revision of an over thousand-year trial, after which we are supposed to be robbed of our legacy and forced into a straight-jacket in which the most noble limbs of our body grow deformed.

The race of ancestors, their language, their nationality, their spiritual-moral bearing is still alive within us. All attempts to eradicate this could not take hold. We extract from this priceless good quality, stretching far back into prehistory and highly durable, important yardsticks to measure the inner value of cultural accomplishments.

What has sprouted from the old and genuine essence and agrees with it, we prefer. But we do not want something old, rather something unconditionally new, which can also still pass the check test: the test of correctness. Our new thing must also agree with our better insight and with reality. For the researching of this reality and the energetic determination to also follow what has been recognized through research likewise belongs to the decisive aim abilities of the Nordic race.

Classification

We are hence willing to prove whatever can somehow be proven, to present evidence where it can suffice. But evidence does not reach to the ultimate, and it is unfathomable. It lives within us, and we act according to it, and all evidence and reasons have in it their ultimate reason.

National Socialism is a worldview, it is also even more. It was possible that hundreds gave their lives for it, thousands their blood, and hundreds of thousands again stand ready for it at any moment. Blood sacrifice, as is known, is not yet proof of the truth, but an infallible proof of the obligation to something ultimate, eternal. The devotion to die for an idea continues in the readiness to live for it and tests itself in the ability to transform it into the deed despite all the dullness and obstacles of daily life.

The racial and folkish idea of National Socialism also gives this strength. It does not give it, because it is thought, rather because it is lived, known, believed, wanted. So, it rests and works as union inside.

To portray it outwardly, we first find out the fundamental thing, in that we trace the connection of culture and heredity, the roots of our fate and of our freedom.

Then we broaden our view from our closest environment, of homeland and the love for it, to the world historical and idea historical view to illuminate from there the moving questions of our present.

Third, we discuss how education on a racial and folkish foundation is to be established, so that what is already now possible and the path into the future become visible.

Finally, we weigh against each other: faith, science, and desire.

CHAPTER

2

HEREDITY, RACE, NATIONALITY & CULTURE

We speak of race, if a larger group of individual beings within their species agree in the special and balanced constitution of many and precisely the most important genes, and hence in the characteristics and traits in which the genes show themselves. Corresponding to the unity of body and soul, it is about the physical and psychological characterizes, and in man, whose soul produces spiritual and moral forces, also about the spiritual and moral and about the genes that determine this. Race is hence so comprehensive that many sciences are involved in researching and portraying the various sides of its essence, its physical and its psychological, spiritual, moral, its meaning in the present and its working in the past.

Race is an object of natural science, in whose sphere, above all, the physical characteristics and traits belong. Natural science must indeed not ignore the psychological characteristics, they are just not its actual and chief object. However, in man, in whom the psychological characteristics escalate to high intellectual accomplishments, the science of man is joined by (psychological) anthropology, the science of his soul, psychology, and genetics erects a wide bridge between the physical and the psychological, in that it also examines the heredity of psychological characteristics and abilities and the hereditary factors for them.

Race is especially an object of natural history. The heredity of the physical characteristics of race reaches far back, to the time in which the race formed itself. Those are long periods of times, during which the race passed down genes unchanged and even given race-mixing again and again dominated. These processes are natural processes, and their course occupies natural history.

Race is an object of the Science of the Arts, for psychological, intellectual-moral characteristics are tied to the physical characteristics. The psychological (intellectual and moral) constitution and bearing correspond to the physical manifestation, and this psychological aspect is also inherited. But the Science of the Arts examines and treats the psychological content. Insight into the physical aspect of race is likewise necessary for it, however, as a natural science prerequisite.

Race is especially an object of the history of ideas, for the intellectual-moral characteristics of the races have showed themselves in their historical accomplishments, and the history of ideas treats these cultural accomplishments of the most diverse kind.

The natural scientific and natural historical significance of race becomes visible almost only among animals, among which the intellectual only here and there, as onset, becomes important for our human view. In terms of the Science of the Arts and the history of ideas, the intellectual-moral significance of race steps into the foreground in man and in the escalation of human accomplishments to nationality and culture. We can dissect folks into their racial elements and discover in nationalities and cultures the diverse inner general attitude of the races involved in them. If this dissection (analysis) is successful, then it must conversely be possible to construct, explain and understand the folks, their nationalities, and cultures from their racial elements through composition (synthesis) again as well.

Racial Property

The genes in which the members of a race must agree so that the race exists at all determine through the characters and accomplishments that grow from them the value of this race. These characteristics and accomplishments can hence be designated as racial properties.

Regarding the activity of these racial properties, a basic difference now separates man from the animals, not merely from the mammals closest to him such as the anthropoid apes, rather also from those living in state similar organizations such as bees, ants, or termites: The life of animals is almost only instinct regulated and the individual leads its special existence even in the herd or in the animal state. There is hardly teaching and learning. Drive life in man is almost totally elevated into consciousness. The drives to imitate, to communicate, to help and to be important have thrived to unexpected strength and take effect in awareness of accomplishments that to lead to it that the individual is never isolated, rather communicates with others through gesture and language, later through writing as well, receives experiences from others and adds his own, passes on this property from generation to generation and finally even becomes conscious of his history within the framework of the community.

The bird builds its nest purely instinctively, even if it has never yet seen one. Likewise, the actions of the ants are integrated purely instinctively and without even the slightest communication. A brood of young ants builds the same construction that corresponds to its species. The direction by oldsters, by the example of the existing structures, is probably unnecessary for it, although among this or that state-forming insect structures exist that are strongly reminiscent of human culture: a kind of language, pets, slaves, gardens and fields, narcotics, burial, and such. But man must always learn almost everything anew and remain, if one artificially keeps him away from the legacy of his nationality, far behind even the most primitive folks and cannot speak on his own. What he is, he owes to the gained experiences and institutions of the others, of his clan, of his tribe, of his folk and of the other folks with which his folk have exchanged such experiences and institutions. The psychological, also the spiritual traits which he has inherited, guarantee him a share in this treasure only where he comes to gain it; but then he can also increase it and pass in on enriched.

The acquisition of valuable results is tradition. It leads to it that one uses what the other has found that the new generations stand on the shoulders of the predecessors.

To the bee belongs its honeycomb constructed of hexagonal cells, to the spider belongs its eight-spoke web, to the birds their tendency to their nests, to the fox his house and to the folks belong their racially determined native tribe constitutions, their economic forms, their living manner, their pets, their utensils, weapons and clothes, their language, their art, literature and science, their religious life and their whole culture built upon these details.

Culture is always the result of long-lasting, constantly continued, and increased tradition. Each contribution to this increase and escalation, each discovery, invention, and improvement, but also every passing along of the already found, is a cultural deed and presupposes a perpetrator, somebody who bears these cultural accomplishments, that means creates, has, passes on a culture-bearer.

The relationship between culture-bearer and cultural deed, between achieved and achievement, is the one between gene and application of this biological tendency.

Only a Julius Robert Mayer could enrich the knowledge of the laws of inanimate nature with the comprehensive law of the preservation of energy, only a Gregor Mendel our knowledge of the laws of animate nature with the laws of heredity, only a Goethe our literature with his Faust, only a Hitler our folk with his national unification.

Quite specific genes in a fortunate union are necessary for accomplishments of the highest kind, which, however, are always only possible and can also only have a fruitful effect, if they have been preceded by many small and medium accomplishments, in part by the great men themselves, but more so by others. For even the great thing wants to be earned and could never become tangible to the others if their own effort did not meet it half-way. Anticipating and paving the way; but even the average accomplishments of a peasant bound to the soil, of an asset work of the productive worker, of a conscientious official, rests on the very substantial genes of these culture-bearers and their predecessors.

Each cultural accomplishment results from such genes, biological tendencies and the characteristics growing out of them, and the value of cultural accomplishment is the yardstick for the value of the characteristics upon which they rest. The characteristics, however, are tied to the race and hence represent a racial property, and the cultural accomplishments, the result, are, since they only remain valuable, if they are passed on, tradition properties. One calls the passing along, the handing down, often enough even itself an inheritance. One should think of Goethe's: *"What you have inherited from your fathers, acquire it, in order to possess it."* All cultural property is in this sense cultural legacy. This manner of expression has its good right. A tradition property is only handed down if genes are there that are fitting for it. If they are lacking, then the legacy becomes forgotten, the cultural property decays.

Racial Properties of First & Higher Order

Our view of the concept' legacy has changed under the influence of the doctrine of genetics.

Earlier, one designated as legacy from all the properties, house, farm, and possessions of the testator. That aside from these materials goods also physical-psychological traits and characteristics are inherited from the parents, in which these traits express themselves, one noted only occasionally, and accordingly one used the word *"legacy"* for it only in the figurative sense.

Today we know the significance of the passing along of biological tendencies and the characteristics resulting from them through the fertilized egg, and the blood-bound kind of legacy has become the actual one for us. If one speaks of inheritance of house, farm, and property, that hence now logically seems to us as the figurative meaning.

This change of the meaning of the word *"inheritance"* and of all words derived from it away from external goods and assets to those inside the owners, preservers, and multipliers of these goods, which is the prerequisite for all possession, preservation, and multiplication, is an important achievement of a new time. For it is a shift of the intellectual-moral weight from the effect to the essence-based cause.

But both physical property and the intellectual possessions, among which we now speak of inheritance only in the figurative sense, are tied to their bearers.

Raw materials as well and even the ore deposits of a mine are only goods insofar and only have their value where human beings exist who can process these materials and who master the very ingenious process of extraction and utilization.

Or a hereditary farmstead and everything that goes with it is indeed material property, but rules something spiritual-moral whose expression is this material property, and which again and again declares itself for the sensible observer in it. The same is true for the spiritual goods of culture; they as well point at the nature and valuable characteristics of their creators and bearers.

Material property and the spiritual goods of culture, both are as inherited goods, the result of the genes and characteristics of the bearers of these inherited goods. So that the cultural goods can be created, preserved, increased, blood-tied characteristics are required. Without these characteristics, the cultural goods would not exist, could not be preserved, and increased.

The valuable, cultural-creative characteristics of the culture-bearers are the foundation; the inherited goods, their products, build upon them. So, it is justified to designate the respective supply of gene-based characteristics as racial properties of the first order and the tradition values as racial properties of higher order.

The racial properties of first and higher order agree in that both are not directly inherited and merely gene determined. Directly inherited is not the characteristic, rather the biological tendency, or expressed more precisely: the manner of reaction, that means the manner how the organism responds to stimuli and demands that confront it, takes a position toward them. Each characteristic and each accomplishment are such a response that it gives, such a position that it takes. That is simultaneously the still unconscious preliminary stage of valuation and value creation, which given increased mental forces then reaches the conscious stage and high into the intellectual. However, these first and the highest stirrings of valuation and property creation are based on the same primal behavior of body and soul, thus the physical-psychological union of everything living. The subsequent response, the stand taken, has as a result the racial property, and indeed on the still totally unconscious and gene-closest stage of the racial property of first order, the biological tendency based, gene-based characteristic, and then on the higher levels the higher, more conscious, finally very thought out and escalated through the amassing of legacy result of those characteristics and the biological tendencies at work within them, the racial properties of higher order. These tradition properties, the higher the magnitudes they reach among the most highly talented races, strive precisely because of this their high racial gene determination into the unconditional, commonly valid, and from their environmental condition into the objectively demanded, the necessary. The validity extracted from the actual then finally characterizes the racial properties of highest order, of which we will still speak.

The racial properties of the higher (and highest) order are the constantly increasing result of the racial goods of the first order and build upon them as preliminary stage, like, say, the stories and roof of a house upon the foundation walls and cellar rooms. The roof lies *"higher"*, but it is not *"better"* than the cellar, one belongs to the other, and everything collapses without the supporting foundation.

The relationship of a note to its higher notes can provide another comparison. They sound in as soon as the note is struck and determine its tone hue. Similarly, the racial properties of higher order that join in as soon as the racial properties of the first order take effect in the culture-bearers, determine the unique stamp of the culture. But the higher notes are not therefore something *"higher"* or *"better"*, and they could never exist on their own.

But any such comparison can illustrate only one part of the thing itself, and this is only insufficiently; for they are comparisons from the sphere of inanimate nature (house, string), while the result that the racial properties of the first order produce in the racial properties of higher order is a process in animate nature, a life process, and possesses its incomparable uniqueness. Other life processes as well cannot further illustrate it, and that is not at all necessary; one must adhere to it oneself.

To justify the distinction between racial properties of first and higher order, it is also unnecessary that one now begin, say, to provide cultural accomplishments with order numbers. Even without that, for example, the steam plough is an accomplishment of a higher order than the wheel plough, and this is compared to the simple, original hook plough. One could posit such series everywhere and illustrate what it meant by the higher order.

Divergence of Tradition From Heredity

The racial properties of first order rest on the biological tendencies being causally inherited; the gene pool that enters the fertilized egg is exactly determined by the heredity process and always the same. Then this gene pool must prove itself in growth and life in the environment into which it is placed.

For the transmission of the racial properties of the higher order, tradition, the corresponding thing applies step by step, but the conformity is likewise based in the tie's fact of the traditional property to the inherited characteristics. Exact conformity does not exist, rather also divergence.

The first agreement and simultaneously divergence is regarding heredity and transmission itself.

The racial properties of the first order are elements of their bearers, downright make up them and are hence firmly tied to them. If these bearers just procreate at all, then they necessarily and causally pass along their genes, and thus their racial properties of the first order.

The racial properties of the higher order are no longer so firmly tied to the culture-bearers. If their bearers die, they are also lost, and if their bearers degenerate in their genes, likewise, although usually only after some time as soon as the consequences take effect. But the racial properties of the higher order can also be passed on to bearers of another kind, of another race and of other nationality, if the difference of the borrowers from the creators is not all too great.

What is true for the racial properties of the first order is also similarly true for the racial properties of the higher order, but not the same, and precisely the divergence and the possibilities and dangers that they present are very substantial.

The second agreement and simultaneously divergence is regarding the quantity of what is inherited or passed along.

The genes of the cell at fertilization (aside from isolated plants) cannot be accumulated beyond the prescribed measure. They are tied to the cell strings, and from these, thanks to the so-called cell division, always only half of each supply enters the egg at fertilization. So, it is assured that the fertilized egg always contains the same gene mass and is never overloaded. The racial properties of the first order, the realized genes, are hence firmly limited.

The racial properties likewise cannot be accumulated arbitrarily, rather only corresponding to the holding capacity of their bearers, and thus is limited even in the greatest genius as in all human ability, and this rests on the natural limitation of the racial properties of the first order. But the peculiarity of the culture-creators is that they find means to expand these initially quite narrow borders. They finally develop an education system and all kinds of memory aides and can vastly increase the quantity of what is handed down.

One sees how here as well among racial properties of the higher order, what is true for the racial properties of the first order is roughly repeated, but not exactly, and how important divergence is at the same time. The third agreement and simultaneously divergence regards the life- causal preservation of the inherited or passed along.

The genes respond to the environment with characteristics, the racial properties of the first order. Edelweiss existence means producing in the environment of the high mountains fleshy blossoms and leaves with thick white hairs close to the ground. But Edelweiss existence also means in the environment of the low land losing many of these peculiarities and in blossom and growth roughly approaching the ox- eye daisy.

Plants and animals can usually merely respond to the environment, but not formatively intervene into it themselves, aside from, say, their number. But man can do that, and indeed with the help of his racial properties of the higher order. He responds to his environment not merely with his characteristics, rather also in that he uses them, especially the richly developed mental ones, to carry out culture creations. They rest indeed on the characteristics of the culture bearers, on the racial properties of the first order, but they go far beyond this foundation and enable the culture-bearers to themselves create their own new environment form of their cultural accomplishments.

Man wraps himself in his clothing, builds his own house, cultivates his field, breeds animals; so, he produces his own food, and through the heated room even his own *"climate"* according to his will and decision. A throng of such institutions and inventions, all racial properties of the higher order, now demand as an artificial environment from his genes new, adapted responses and thus confront him with ever more arduous tasks to prove himself.

What among the racial properties of the first order was still almost entirely nature, repeats in the racial properties of the higher order, increased and increasing, yes, even exaggerated as culture.

Durability & Fleetingness of The Racial Properties

In all three cases, if one pays attention to cultural events, the divergences become visibly more important. The eternally nature-causal and inviolate constant lies in the conformities. The racial values of the first order are durable in value, where they are simply just preserved. Increase of value and decrease of value are possible only through accumulation and consumption, through favorable selection, conscious racial policy, populace policy, or conversely through unfavorable race-mixing, below average procreation of the above-average, increase of congenital diseases and such.

In the divergences lies the possibility of greater value change, which can far exceed the value increases and value decreases in the gene pool itself, and which are even able to retroactively subject the gene pool to favorable or ruinously unfavorable conditions. The racial properties of the higher order can lead to unimagined accomplishments, but also to totally unexpected failure.

If races and folks fail already on a low cultural level, then usually valuable genes were simply missing. Their failure at a higher cultural level, however, awakens the impression that the initial success was a kind of blossoming and maturing, the decay a kind of aging and dying off of the races, folks and cultures. One then figures that the one is just as necessary as the other, one cannot promote anything about it and not do anything against it.

But one makes a huge mistake. One can indeed compare the spread of borrowed goods and foreign goods, the exaggerated accumulating of handed down goods, the effeminacy through one's own, exaggerated culture with the accumulation of non-excreted wastes in an organism, back to which the manifestations of aging are traced. But that is merely a comparison and does not go far.

Neither races nor folks, neither anthills nor states are organisms in the genuine sense of the word, which one can apply to them only comparatively. With being an organism goes, for example, that it takes in nourishment, absorbs and it and excretes the wastes, that it grows, that it multiplies either through division or fertilization, and that it has organs that serve these functions. But if folks or states subjugate and absorb other such entities, this is visibly not a taking of food into the stomach, and if states divide or fall, also not procreation.

They are forms of the living together of organisms, but simply not these organisms themselves, like conversely, the so-called cell state is a state only comparatively and, is an organism. What is true for organisms, in no way, needs to be true for races, folks or states. Comparisons should not guide us, rather only reality.

One could only then rightly designate races, folks and even cultures as young or old, if their genes could be young or age. But they are always equally old and always equally young, come from an eternity and are capable on their own of continuing into eternity.

Not because the genes had aged, do folks fail, rather because they do not keep their gene pool pure and take care of their racial properties of the higher order. But precisely in the high cultures, in the wealth of the handed down goods, lies the manifold opportunity to use the freedom that the divergence of legacy from heredity allows us for bad and offers us for good.

The divergences rarely lead to decline, rather contain both possibilities: ruin and vitality.

That the great culture folks previously all eventually took the path of failure and only in the beginning, during their so-called blossoming and maturation, passed the test, does not rest upon a law of nature that one cannot escape.

Many forests perished previously, but that does not lie in the forest's nature, rather in external natural events and incorrect planting and care and preservation. Forests cannot assure this care for themselves, but cultures comprise human beings who can recognize their life conditions and adjust care accordingly. Certainly, this requires a high degree of insight and political will formation.

Both must also be put into action long in and long-term. One generation does not secure the sequence of generations itself in the long run. Only long-term, goal-conscious work reaching across many generations can bring success.

Among the folks of the previous cultures, much of the required will and desire already appeared here and there, but it did not suffice. The Indians saw the decline of their race, but their caste laws were only in part race laws and came too late. The Romans as well saw the desolation of their farms and childlessness, but the laws with which they wanted to counteract this were too weak and were not upheld.

The insight of those times did not penetrate to the true causes of the decline, and the political energy as well no longer steered an alternative course. So, one could not effectively counter the misfortune, neither through race policy and population policy in favor of the racial properties of the first order nor through culture policy in favor of the racial properties of the higher order, and also from them again in favor of the racial properties of the first order and of the genes themselves as their foundation.

The Dangers from the Racial Properties of the Higher Order

In the divergence of legacy from heredity lie compulsion and freedom, ruin, and prosperity; but initially the dangers dominate among these consequences. One must first understand them, before one can go about evaluating the expert uses as well that lie in the possibilities of divergence, and thus our freedom, and finally mastering the dangers themselves. They are foreign influence, accumulation, misdirection.

Foreign Influence

The native tradition of a folk, its own property, directly results from its legacy that grows out of itself and is again activated and affirmed, broadened, and shaped by each new folk comrade. But because the extremely complicated soul of man is thoroughly trainable, he can learn and gain much, even such things that he himself has not sought or found, yes, which attracts him because of its exoticness or is forced upon him by foreigners.

The same thing applies even to the animal to a limited degree. A chimpanzee can ride a bicycle with a mastery that man will hardly ever achieve. But the difference immediately shows itself that he can no longer repair even the slightest damage to the bicycle. His skill lasts only as long as man is there, who maintains the equipment for him.

The Negro still learns to fix the bicycle, but he has not invented it, and it is difficult for him to himself adapt it to new conditions or to improve it. The state is more ingenious that a bicycle, and one has also put this *"tool"* into the hands of the Negroes. Caricatures, like the states in Liberia, Haiti, and San Domingo, were the result, and even that much would not have come about if one could not convey the accomplished examples of our states and without half-breeds.

"Great is every creator; important only through the preserver" (Jahn); merely learned, handed down goods, hence actually foreign property, is usually soon lost. The folks adapt what is really learned to their own nature:

- understood,
- improving,
- enriching,
- misunderstood,
- distorting,
- twisting.

They make it their borrowed property. With time and with the folks, handed down goods often begin long journeys, in the process become re-shaped manifold and they have a re-shaping effect.

Frequently, all kinds of upheavals sweep away the connecting links, and the deception arises as if the various folks had accomplished the same or similar thing independently of each other.

The one half of a comprehensive history of the cultures would have to find out the wandering path and modifications of the borrowed goods and the retention or rejection of foreign property, the other half the points of origin of the native property.

The more native property of an ethnic group that one can discover, the more clearly one can find out its guiding influence in the independent processing of foreign property into borrowed property, the more significant does the tribal essence emerge, and the more clearly does the essence of its culture-bearing racial core reveal itself in it.

The Nordic race is the great example; its world historical significance rests on the wealth of its native property, on the energy with which it independently processes borrowed property and develops it from its essence. But the danger of foreign influence exists for it as well.

Every culture contains a certain measure of foreign property, and it is all the better off, the more it has already improved it, adapted it to its own nature or even overcome it with more developed new creations. No ethnic group can shut itself off from the rest of the world, and if it managed that, it would lose an important source of its strength, namely the altercation with the foreigner.

(Excessive) foreign influence (Überfremdung) is only present if the foreign material that is not processed and cannot be processed becomes so much that even the native threatens to drown in it. One should take language as an example. A few borrowed words, a foreign word here and there, should not yet endanger it. But usually, these intruders are only pacemakers for more. But if the most important basic concepts are always expressed in foreign words, and if these expressions become frequent in the sentences, then the language is already foreign influenced and in danger, and the idea even more much so.

Namely, foreign property then reaches deep into the conceptual, into the moral, into the life bearing and worldview.

*"What is most natural to a folk, because inborn to it
and hence life expression, under circumstances means for
a folk with a different nature not only a grave threatens,
rather even the end."*

- Adolf Hitler.

Accumulation

Seen from our perspective, among native cultures, only a minor growth of cultural property results, and it integrates into the older elements fitting to growth. There cannot yet be much talk of actual accumulation. It also already preconditions the penetration of foreign property, a certain disruption of the native order or even already difficulties to keep it.

But the more cultural property comes together in the cultures of higher level, the sooner do the capacities for comprehension and memory prove themselves too weak for the task arising for them, and one thinks up remedies. Individual folks, for example, the Jews, elevate memorization to an admirable art. Others, such as the Egyptians and Babylonians, relied on ancient times in writing. Organized education and writing even a curriculum, libraries, reference works, a developed educational system, schools of various levels, museums and many other things then enable high cultures a previously unknown stockpiling and handing down of legacies, historical accounts, and cultural accomplishments of every kind, and soon these become so plentiful that the individual can no longer master it.

The professions divide, require their own teaching, and only with effort can schools fulfil their task to select and convey the most important. Everything seems important, the old and the new, the failure and the success, the distant and the near, the foreign and the native; yes, the foreign beckons more and hence also mean more.

The bearers of the culture threaten to suffocate in the native and foreign traditions created and taken ever farther by them.

Is educated if one knows where one should look things up? According to Lagarde, one is educated if one can distinguish between the important and the unimportant. Just what is important? Where does over-stimulated thought still find support? Each word threatens to remain a mere concept, behind which one seeks to grasp a second? In this condition, thought dissolves from things, reason from comprehension. Real capacity for comprehension is replaced by a feigned one, intelligence by intellectualism. No wonder, for the energy of direct will and thought is consumed in the processing of tradition or of individual parts of it. Between man and reality, which he should confront with breast and brow, steps the concept already thought for him, the word, writing, the book. Everything seems already thought, said, taken for granted.

But that is mere appearance. For all human knowledge and human ability, even if it always penetrates farther, is small and only piecemeal, and the still non-researched, unshaped, unfathomed mass remains inexhaustible. But especially in the sciences, one thing builds on the other, and the new knowledge preconditions to a great degree the previously already achieved. So, the accumulated tradition indeed simplifies the more distant steps here as well, but simultaneously makes them harder.

Highly developed cultures can only remain viable if these dangers of suffocation in the accumulated cultural goods are effectively countered.

Misdirection

Cultured man has tamed his pets, his useful plants, his whole environment (cultivated, domesticated), and he has tamed himself as well. But while pets and plants are tended by him, so that his breeding and his protection replace the strict selection of nature, the tamed (cultivated, domesticated) human being only appears to have removed himself a little from this selection; he must, when things get serious, continue to assert himself against his own, his enemies, and nature.

To prove oneself in the natural, uncultivated environment is difficult, for it put its life and death demands pitilessly severe. But the self-created environment comprises nothing but mitigation: better food, better housing, richer life, not so close to death.

This elbowroom, created by beginning culture, is constantly widened, often quickly with its successful development. In it lies all the advantages of culture, but also all alienation from nature and the danger of becoming unsure in the responses which this mitigated its tamed environment demands relentlessly. It is even more treacherous, as the cloaking veil of culture removes these demands from view for long stretches.

One can compare a living creature that asserts itself against its environment through the responses that it gives to it as its characteristics based on its genes to a swimmer struggling against the waves, and the demands of the environment, even the strict selection that it imposes, to turbulent weather and storm. Steering happens through the racial properties of the first order.

Even the racial properties of the higher order steer their bearers onward toward the racial properties of the first order, which work and realize themselves in the cultural creations; yes, their development initially means an important head start for their bearers.

Let us take as an example those racial properties of the higher order which make up crop cultivation. The crop-field nourishes the most capable peasant best. He preserves and protects the peasant virtues through his work, from which crop cultivation grew. Even when other professions are added, the peasantry remains the nourishment profession, the unshakeable support of folk energy for a long time. So far, culture stays toward the racial properties of its creators and protects them.

But it only does that for a stretch. The rural settlement grows, the city emerges. The steam plough of the large landholder threatens the peasant. Those whom he is supposed to nourish can become too many. The other professions can uproot him through taxes and other means of their greed.

Or another case: the trades escalate to industry that destroy the tradesperson. The original direction, as if were, has reversed itself.

The racial properties turn in their escalated forms against their creators. Such manifestations exist in the most diverse areas.

The machine, invented to help with work, one uses it to make people unemployed.

Chemistry supplies poison gases and explosives of unexpected effectiveness.

Contraceptive measures threaten to prevent procreation.

Even medicine turns into harm when it secures more favorable conditions for the sick to reproduce than it does for the healthy.

Adding to the difficulty are:

- First, inflowing foreign goods that the culture-forming energy cannot process into its own goods (borrowed goods), and which then has a decaying effect.

- Second, the paralysis of the culture-forming energy itself, since the new growth of cultural goods no longer grows properly, professions and strata of the folk get jumbled together, whole groups sink more frequently than individual ones rise, a mass uprooted in its property and upper stratum uprooted in its ideals endanger the spiritual, moral existent of the whole. The accumulation of tradition goods gets out of hand, and judgment, the identification of the important, of the vital, becomes ever more difficult.

- Third, an effeminacy of a cultured man through his cultural institutions, which enrich his life of feeling, broaden his knowledge, beautify his existence, but all too easily paralyze his decisiveness down to the bone.

It is as if the creations of culture had become independent, as if the culture-bearers had lost their mastery over them, even though they are still able to ever increase and perfect the accomplishment itself, and as if the cultural institutions rebelled against their creators.

The racial goods of the higher order steer the culture through the environment effect that develops them no longer toward the racial properties of the first order, rather the steering first becomes unsure through them and then turns into the opposite, into misdirection, and threatens to destroy the flagging bearers of heritage themselves.

The Bolshevist Lunacy & Our Culture-Political Will

If one ponders these dangers, one could conclude: only from the decline of the high cultures could again sprout a new cultural creation, a new beginning, excessive foreign influence could only be overpowered, the ballast of all too highly piled tradition only cast off, the culture-harming environment effect of exaggerated cultural achievements only be overcome, through a thorough destruction of existing culture and through a new construction from the foundation up and with all that freedom and impartiality that must result, if one is not bound by any restricting and burdening past.

That would be an extermination of all traditions, such as Bolshevism wants. One torches the house to get rid of the bugs. It is not, say, a lack of daring that makes us reject such criminal experiments. Rather, they are senseless and futile, because the new start would be purchased through the loss of all the experiences of the past and through the extermination of the bearers of these experiences and institutions, who stand by their cultural goods and would have to be destroyed with them to make room for the dreamed renewal.

This would be a repetition of the already achieved, and the old dangers would exist with it as well. But they could not set it at all. For the destruction of the culture-bearers must lead to the loss of culture. The destruction of precisely that blood from which alone the valuable could grow again is inherent within it. The cultural soil would then be killed, any hope gone.

Hence, it would mean cowardly and criminally withdrawing from the tasks that these dangers from the cultural properties of the higher order put to us if one chooses the destruction of culture and its bearers as a desperate escape. But there is no reason at all for desperation, for each of the named dangers, as soon as it is recognized in its essence, can also be dammed up again and overcome.

The Overcoming of The Dangers

Each of the possibilities for the divergence of tradition from heredity is not merely a danger, rather also a gift and part of our grace if we only know how to use it correctly. We can learn, teach, pass along, we can stockpile experiences, keep knowledge, take applications from it, we can, even if only within very modest boundaries, look ahead and shape world and fate; we have creative energies, memory beyond our individual life in tradition and the talent to consciously employ all of this.

Hence, we will also do it, in that we:

1. expand the native,
2. make the important dominant,
3. correctly steer ourselves from our environment.

Expansion of The Native

Every culture absorbs foreign goods from the outside, but also gives its own goods to the outside. It only remains leading where it can assert itself toward the absorbed and where it can offer the folks around it something decisive.

Advantages and disadvantages lie in both, and it is important to use the advantages and to counter the disadvantages. One should learn wherever one can learn, but should also distinguish whether it is about valuable, superfluous, or even dangerous things, and what effect it will have in the own folk nature. The worst thing is imposed by foreigners; one should think about opium in China.

Even with native property, one should be careful about how one handles it. The most precious thing is the people themselves. Indo-Germanic man, Germanic man, then Europe's folks, then we Germans have through emigration suffered heavy losses and gained little from the foreign foundations not guided by plan. The cultures of the Nordic race have indeed conquered the world, but the Nordic folks have almost bled dry.

When Greek culture, through Alexander's campaign, poured into the orient, the decline of Greek kingdom was no longer to be stopped. Germanic man learned from the Romans to assert himself and win against superior weaponry, military leadership, administration, and defeated Rome. Charlemagne, the Frank emperor, had to forbid the export of German swords to the Slavs.

But all Europe's folks have given their weapons, even their intellectual ones, their science, their technology, in part in joy to be their teachers, in part in competition for base, race-betraying profit and in short-sighted underestimation of the danger. These folks are already rising and turning against their benefactors. Not being complaisant in adoption, reserved in giving, in both considering the consequences, that will protect against harm, will elevate reputation, solidify self-esteem. Only seldom does something let itself be made reversible. Instead, one must add new layers to abolish the old ones again, where that is necessary and desirable. The prerequisite is that one finds the strength, above all, even the political strength, to put the native in the center and to logically expand where it is still capable of such an expansion.

Every culture contains an unexpected quantity of still unused creative possibilities. One must learn to find and exploit them. That way, one pushes out the foreign the fastest. Only this procedure secures the superiority as well, while all mere opposition simultaneously makes the opponent dependent. The struggle against the foreign word, for example, remains hopeless, if the foreign words are merely supposed to be Germanized and not instead language-creative energies are freed up which led to a new, independent expression of the idea.

One should not let oneself become annoyed, because many of these attempts do not work right away; for it is about the grains of seed that sprout. It is like the effort to replace foreign raw materials with native ones. They must not remain substitutes, and not every attempt succeeds. Yes, one can even deceive oneself regarding need. Many foreign goods are worth a lot, but like tobacco are better off absent.

The shaping of the native will frequently begin with a return to the native. Only one must be clear that the old cannot be repeated, rather should merely give a stimulus for the new. In things of culture, there are no repetitions. Everything past stands on an earlier level, but everything's future, according to its beginnings, is still under the totally different conditions of the present. The old has again and again been the teacher for the new. The great example overall is the Renaissance.

It is unnecessary that the old present itself to the later generation in superior perfection to stimulate it to new creations. Even modest beginnings, lovingly undertaken, can contribute something important for the higher level. In that Luther looked at how the folk talked, he gave the German language a decisive push forward. Inner value can exist even without outer splendor. Buried beginnings of Germanic antiquity that today gain validity again are, for example: the leader and the following, male loyalty, honoring the ancestors and love for the clan, the hereditary farmstead.

Often enough, the foreign has crowded out something native and very imposing, which could have continued in another direction, for example, among us the end rhyme and the staff alliteration. This and Germanic verse structure was highly appropriate for our language, which stresses the meaning-bearing syllables, while the end rhyme and the new poetry of the south inflict great violence upon it. Here as well, there is no return to the old, but indeed very important opportunities for something new, something again appropriate for our language. Richard Wagner and others have taken up the alliteration again here and there, and if such experiments gain room, the guide back to the original inner bearing, which alone is what matters; the form is only serving means.

Many foreign goods seem harmless and secondary, say some allegedly indispensable foreign word or a foreign fashion. But the fundamental stands even behind the secondary fashion include lipstick and fingernail polish, the cigarette, jazz and much else, and if such things gain the upper hand, the German woman and German social life suddenly have an alien face.

Usually, foreign powers are then also at play, like with import from across the sea, foreign commerce, or, with wine, Rome from ancient times, which is why already the Germanic tribe of the Sweben tried to ban the import of wine.

But it went deeper when Roman law came to Germania and the new religion. Both examples show, followed through the history of the Holy Roman Empire of the German Nation and the German religious wars, how such borrowed goods can also have the highest political importance and can grow into a folk's foundations. For that, the foreigners do not even have to first enter the land in numbers. But if they do that and claim, like among us the Jews, even dominance, then one must with calm firmness return them to the limits of right and fairness.

Determination of The Essential

The expansion of the native continues itself in the determination of the essential. The faith in the future replaces the obligation toward the past.

The fertilized egg receives only so much in its new life as is necessary; not the body that it should build for itself, already in miniature, rather the main thing: the basic traits of the later arrangement, its melody plus a little nourishment. It resembles a backpack packed with the strictest thrift, in which the order to march is the main thing.

The heir of a culture must also ask himself: how do I pack my backpack? It is extremely small, the cultural goods overwhelmingly manifold. The most important thing here as well are the basic traits of the order itself. Some spiritual trail food is likewise necessary, but just enough so that the order can begin with it, which is brought along as melody and is that of all the life that develops from this good, and which later consumes what is necessary for spiritual nourishment, of knowledge, always according to requirement and overfeeding is avoided.

This is true for every culture-close person newly born into his culture, and it is true for the culture overall. It must maintain its sleekness and cast-off clinkers. Only the unshakeable faith in the future gives it the strength to free itself from the appendages of the past that has accumulated over tradition.

Accumulation of cultural goods means the essential was buried by much that is inessential, not merely by superfluous or dangerous foreign goods, rather also by many remnants and side-effects of its own cultural work. The additions, which did not follow proper growth, are hence to be sorted out. The view is to be opened for what, growing properly, belongs together. Only the latter is important, and in that one determines it, it becomes distinguishable from the unimportant. This work consists simultaneously in a continuing use and an increasing strengthening of the power of judgment.

More important than passing down through teaching and writing is the passing down through the existing institutions of the folk whole. These are what is direct, the other is merely deduced. Yet one should not underestimate it. Science, art. Literature, writing again and again gives culture its direction from what has already been accomplished, in the good and in the bad.

Institutions must stand out according to their importance for the whole: the constitution, the professions and strata of the folk, the manifold dividing occupations and their duties. Specialization in the occupations is necessary, but it should not happen for the sake of the specialists, rather make the whole more structured, controllable. The whole must become visible ethnically graphically in the meaningful gradation of its elements at festivals, processions, and similar occasions. Through their striving upward, toward the whole, the fields and occupations must meet half-way the structure of the whole from below. In every field, in every occupation, in every special branch of knowledge and action, the whole shines and presents itself inside it, if it is nurtured from the ground up. It is so much better controlled from the inside than from the outside through the imprinting of a mass of knowledge that soon escapes memory again. A "general (merely encyclopedic) education" that wants to consider everything, but treats nothing thoroughly and uproots people, gives little benefit.

Knowing a lot does not teach, having reason - said already the profound thinker Heraclitus of Ephesus. Certainly, he also said: Wisdom-loving men must be knowledgeable of many things. Weighing both sayings against each other leads to the essence of true education.

Schools must orient themselves. The material to be taught must be limited to the essential and the instruction so improved that it strengthens the power of judgment, the meaning for the whole. Technical special training should be moved from the schools to the occupations.

Genuine humanity roots itself at the place due it through nationality, homeland, and talent, and draws from this its best energy and grows from here out of inner maturity with purified will also most surely into the communality, insofar this is given to it. So, the indigenous man can preserve his freshness and everything that was achieved before him will be available to him and promote him when he needs it, instead of hindering him., he will let himself be guided by the example of the great cultural accomplishments of the past that have emerged from related blood and by the ideal picture of a purified and firm culture of the German future.

Environment Shaping
For the Security of the Culture-Bearing Race

It is about turning the steering wheel and holding a firm course from a well-understood past through a calm present into the future of the most distant generations. We do not need to let ourselves be driven by the environment effect of our cultural goods, rather we can intentionally employ them as environment to steer ourselves again toward our culture-bearing racial properties.

The racial properties of the higher order, used in this manner, are an important means to put the racial properties of the first order in order again as well, yes, if one looks closely, they are the only means that stand at our disposal for this purpose; but fortunately, this means already suffices, thanks to the progress of our knowledge.

To the racial properties of the higher order belong namely also all the knowledge of the laws of genetics and of the distribution of genetic characteristics in the population. Applying this knowledge, for example, along the path of population-policy legislation, means giving them environment effect and bringing out the improvement of the condition of the racial properties of the first order. Racial properties of the higher order, this time the results of the doctrine of genetics and population science, are employed to steer the racial properties of the first order.

The creations of art have a similar environmental effect as the products of science and their technical applications. The ideal picture of man that they present to our eyes, making motives actions, reaches into the feeling and viewing of people. If art loses itself to false ideals, then it no longer has any at all, then it has a decaying effect; but if it gives them the drive for new life-promoting ideals, then it recruits for them, and the racial goods of the high and highest order, the works of art that they create, again serve the purpose of steering the healing of the racial properties of the first order. Finally, the economy can be employed especially effectively. If it keeps house with the import of dispensable wares, then it makes us dependent and consumes our energy in favor of the others; if it tries to make do with that we have and shuts off false requirements, then it leads us back to ourselves again.

If it guides itself according to the greedy spirit, then it destroys the life of many and of precisely the best inherited goods and culture bearers. Conversely, if it works from the productive spirit, then it builds up, and the entangled system of racial properties of the higher order, which every economy represents, likewise has the effect of steering in favor of the racial properties of the first order.

If we shape our entire culture so that the foreign is pushed back, the native becomes guideline, then the slogan *"open the path for the capable"* first gets its real meaning; for only he will now be capable, whose character lies in the direction that we must wish, so that the folk whole becomes uniform and elevated. And the same is true for the concept of performance. For there as well, we do not simply mean performance, say some record without inner content, rather solely such performances that aim at the overall goal.

The Racial Properties of The Highest Order

The more it is possible to make the racial properties of the higher order, the insights conquered over culture, useable for the steering of the racial properties of the first order, the more decisively the uncertainty is overcome that could result from the divergence of tradition from heredity.

The security that now returns rests on the truth content of the employed insights and knowledge. But so that these were won and prospered so far, required an intellectual work continued through many generations, in which each new result rests upon the earlier one. Hence, it will be appropriate to designate as racial properties of the highest order these highly escalated insights and knowledge that already stretch deep into the area of truth.

They include, above all, the solutions to social questions according to the principles of morality, then the creations of the arts, of the visual ones and of literature, finally scientific knowledge. The prominent politician has such a strong share in all these groups of racial properties of the highest order that he finds the solution to his tasks. Basically, already every, even the simplest cultural achievement, preconditions some insights and knowledge, but there is a vast difference, whether one still depends on experimenting or is already beyond that.

On the level of testing out, success or failure decide over right and wrong afterward, the objects whose existence is at stake give the answer themselves. It is not always sufficiently certain, and one must learn to laboriously differentiate between apparent and real success. - But our insight can also extend so far that we do not have to judge at the end after the result of the success, rather can predict the success already in advance, because we master the conditions under which it set in. Previously, the object provided the answer, and we would have known it precisely, then we would not have had to ask it any longer. Now, on the higher level, we provide it ourselves, and indeed in that we think it out in advance in strict contact with the object. Truth comprises the strict contact and the agreement of thought with the object.

Truth does not deduce its validity from the success, and even the practical applications that it allows can merely display their value for certain, but not prove the truth as truth. There are also truths without visible uses. Yes, truth can occasionally even be harmful for people who are not up to it and lies apparently useful for a stretch. Also, benefits and damages change abruptly, according to the conditions, and have degrees. But the truth exists unchanged, even though new truths go beyond the old ones, and it is valid without gradations.

The relationship toward truth finding is very diverse among folks and cultures. Many have hardly taken any steps in it, others brought decisive things to light, in part in their social institutions, in part in their art, the fewest in science, which was reserved almost only for the folks of Nordic race. But once found, grasped, and obligated, the good, beautiful, genuine grips not only and obligate the people of the race who have found it, rather also others far beyond it, even if finding and going along in the understanding have their racially determined boundaries.

The power of the Nordic race to feel and think its way into the highest accomplishments of even foreign and racially foreign determined cultures is unique; the other races follow it in this in very diverse intervals. In it, tied to the strength to appreciate the foreign in its ultimate values, is the strength to lead in accomplishment in its native law, in art, in science, and to devote itself to them, and indeed to an extent which the other races have remained far behind.

The direction in which the racial properties of such highest unconditional validity must be sought is, however, a matter of the special, racially determined talent, which can often be quite diverse even among Europe's racially so closely related folks. So, we see how a Newton and a Leibniz, independent of one another, in the service of similar research tasks escalate the synthetic method of observation, while two Frenchman, like Descartes with his analytical geometry and Galois with his group theory and its application to the fundamental principle of algebra, advance in the sense of analytical thought.

Hence, even in mathematics, the talents of folks express themselves, and not merely personal ones. The infinitesimal calculus and analytical geometry are valid totally independent of the beings who are, say, capable of grasping them, and the same as for mathematics also applies to the natural sciences and their technical applications, where it is about the ability to grasp and to dominate reality.

The social sciences as well open the view to facts, fathoming of essence and practical application. Here, for example, the application of the concept of race points to the side of analytical talent, that of the concepts of nationality and culture to the side of synthetic talent, and it is again to be noted that a Frenchman, Gobineau, was the pioneering racial theoretician, even though a German like Arndt had already preceded him there in important realizations and another like Woltmann become leading in it.

Again and again, it is the Nordic race that has created the sciences, knowledge, applications, and the preliminary work and accomplishment of other races in the same and every other direction were minor, measured against the accomplishment of the Nordic race. Only to it and the racial properties of the first order tied to it is it given to create racial properties of the higher and highest order with this energy and as a foregone conclusion, which ultimately also stretches into the area of the genuine and discards everything conditional, which otherwise attaches itself to it, so much that they achieve unconditional validity, even though they admittedly remain dependent on their bearers and dry out as soon as they perish.

Freedom & Cultural Technology

Genes are fate. Their application and development, however, elevates itself above fate and juts into the realm of freedom. The products finally, which the racial properties of the first order to bring into the racial properties of the higher and highest order, make us free, if we apply them correctly and make sure that they continue to work according to the law from which they have been breed, according to the law of the spirit of our own nationality and the culture-bearing race determining it.

For the freedom for which we strive does not comprise us renouncing our own folk's essence, rather of fulfilling it. We want to finally be, and be allowed to become, those who we already always were, and we want the freedom to act accordingly.

The insights according to which the dangers of high culture are banished and being able to move the forces that work in the wrong direction into the right one, demand that we develop a conscious cultural technology.

Culture is not something that we must let drift and accept just as it comes. Rather, it is our duty to nurture it according to the best knowledge and conscience and with world-historical responsibility.

It is also correct that the great cultural accomplishments always emanate from talented individuals, who do not let themselves be arbitrarily compelled, but it is likewise correct that very much can happen to prepare the paths for the emergence and working of such talents.

A substantial number of our greatest geniuses were not the first or second, rather later children of their parents. If the one child system becomes a common custom, then the talents that can lie in children born later are lost to the nation. Promotion of child-rich, congenitally healthy families thus also means an increase in the appearance's probability of brilliant talents.

One must not have exaggerated impressions about the ability of a talent to develop under adverse conditions. Although personality grows from obstacles, it likewise needs the preconditions favorable to it; time will never be equally ripe for them, but they must mature toward it. For where nothing ripens, even the best farmer cannot harvest.

Many, and precisely the most important, men were the fulfilment of long harbored yearnings. So apparently an extraordinary lot lies in us awakening the right yearnings, so that men grow up who can fulfil them.

Indeed, the laws of nature are necessary and universally valid, and we also stand under them. But all technology shows that we can also apply these laws according to our need and will. In this application, we are free. The momentary laws of decline are valid only for as long as we endure them.

CHAPTER

3

WORLD HISTORICAL & SCIENTIFIC VIEW

All cultural technology is simultaneously cultural policy, and cultural policy the highest, if not basically the solely imaginable kind of politics at all. For politics is goal-driven action in the service of an idea. It does not satisfy itself with the world as it is, rather; it wants to make it better.

That all kinds of incurable, immature world redeemers have brought into disrepute the serious and purified will to make it better should not deceive us. *"Doesn't matter, do it better!"* says Tölpelhans in the fairy-tale, when he surveys his damage afterward, and the next time he does it even worse - because he is simply Tölpelhans (a blockhead). We are guided by the idea, the view of the real and of its laws and the duty we receive from it. In the Edda, it is written in the great poem"The Prophetess's View" (Wöluspa): Evil gets better, Baldur returns home. We do not believe in Baldur, but we understand the deep meaning of these words: How should Balder, the symbol of right and peace, return home if we let evil proliferate from aversion toward improvement? And how should he return home? That means right and peace return to us, if we do not prepare the site for them through our work?

Politics in this sense must not limit into the world, rather it must also start with the human being, and it must not be satisfied with the human being, rather it must also take care of the process of heredity process. For that, it must evaluate the hereditary characteristics, and it can only do that from the vantage point of folk and race. Not the human being as general concept can guide it, rather only Nordic man, capable of leading, according to the demonstration of his world-historical accomplishment, to racial properties of the highest order, and there as well not one floating in the clouds, rather the German rooted in his folk.

Whoever has clearly and compellingly seen a condition to be possible and the path to reach it, will invest everything to realize as much of this view, of this idea, as he can. That is our improving. For after struggle and work, we want genuine peace.

Hence, the ideal attitude toward the future, toward our inner future as well, must root in the grasp of reality such as it presents itself now.

But each present has become and first becomes understandable as one that has become.

History continues the brief experiences of the just now living generation in great distances, where much that is now very manifold and entangled still lies there simple, and where conditions and processes that seem like the present ones, if one thinks about them more deeply, enlighten, warn, instruct us and school our comprehension, solidify our will. History shows how what is becoming so - how it easily could have turned out totally different - what value it has - and how one can make it better again. One's own life teaches much, the history of the whole folk infinitely more, but only world-history can show us world-historical goals.

Hence the view of the past, of the world from which we come, the view of the present, the world in which we live, and the view of the future, the world we want to enter, our idea, together inseparable. This third or, more accurately, first step awakens enthusiasm, the second sobers up, the historical clarifies, and only all three together provide the whole and secure that orientation-bearing (Gesinnungshaltung) from which the politician or cultural technician again and again adapts his measures and can resolutely apply the knowledge.

It is superfluous to discuss what must exist first, that three-fold view or the orientation-bearing that goes with it; for one depends on the other.

The view remains useless if the right orientation does not accommodate it or let itself be awakened from it, and the orientation remains unsuccessful if it lacks the overview where it should employ itself.

The orientation-bearing can be the impulse to conquer the view, and it was that among the pioneers of the folkish idea, who traced the path of the Nordic race from its origins on up to us and from that only based what their heart had already previously felt.

Conversely, however, this view can also again awaken the bearing where it still slumbers, say, and in the completeness and wealth in which it can today already be established, it is simultaneously the strongest impulse to use it and to follow it.

Finally, view and orientation require the support knowing that is to be prepared and correctly applied to find the path to realization. Without that, the whole great effort would be pitifully wasted.

Homeland & Love

The orbit, in which the individual is rooted and from which he grows into the whole of the German nationality, is his homeland. It is defined in terms of landscape, dialect, tribe membership.

In the broader sense, the German homeland is the land in which the German tribes settle, of which they took possession working and which they have turned, according to their will, into what it is.

Once it was a mere environment; but they cleared the forests, drained the swamps, constructed roads. They have imprinted the land with the stamp of their nature, where that was previously possible, and with the means that their talent put at their disposal. The environment has become homeland and becomes it ever more so.

The psychological connections of the inhabitants to their land become even more passionate, the more the external and internal reshaping and development proceeds toward homeland. Each feels from his surroundings the work, sweat and blood of his ancestors coming to meet him, and since the accomplishments of man rest on his tradition, the jointly experienced history as well, which has placed the same demands all and has formed a uniform authentication and valuation, is something equalizing, binding.

Only on the soil of the homeland and before the claim of history does a folk solidify from its landscapes and tribes into that deep inner union that one calls nationality, and which always has as a prerequisite that a race dominates leading and gives to all a common basic direction reinforced and confirmed by the common possessions of the land and of the history.

Only the multiple voices of the races represented in the German folk, standing close together, tied by blood and tied by fate, the diversity of the German tribes, the manifoldness of the landscapes and narrower homelands, gives German essence its full strength and greatness.

The ultimate units upon which it rests are seen from the vantage point of the folk, the family, seen from the vantage point of the German homeland, the home. The will for the whole immediately bursts its apparent narrowness and limitation; and the force of political will formation, which today roars across Germany unifying under the sign of the ancient swastika, also creates new forms of action of the narrower homeland, of the tribes, of the provinces, for the great idea of blood and soil, race, and folk. The work service at the Party Day in Nuremberg, the peasants at Bückeberg are the ultimate symbols for it. Each of these thousands and hundreds of thousands stands for home and homeland like the Wehrmacht does for the whole folk.

But where does this force come from, and where goes it want to go? The meaning of the word home can lead us to it. Home is the settlement, the farmstead, and its surroundings in contrast to everything Strange that pushes against it, and the word home itself is related to the Greek word for sleeping place. The home is the place where one lies one's head to rest and conceive one's children, and where many generations before us have already done the same thing. The cradles of the children and the graves of the dead both belong to home and homeland.

Among us, much has been spoken and written about the homeland. We have homeland study, homeland science, homeland history. One puts ethnology and prehistory in the homeland's service idea. But this is not capable of a major deepening.

We build homesteads for German man, the German family. Without that, the idea of folk and race would lack the fulfilling deed. It locates the settlement above all in the country, where there is still room, and seeks temporary solutions in the city. The congenitally healthy family must fill its home with German cultural content. Permanence and homeland feeling can grow only on such a basis.

Above the local stands, then stands the German one. It receives its blood-tied meaning, determined by the work of the generations, German history. This, the succession of generations, the graves of prehistory, leads back to the Germanic settlement, and then again to the Indo-Germanic one and to the great cultural creations of the Indo-Germanic folks even far beyond the European region.

Prehistory as well never lets itself be limited to the narrower homeland. The pre-historical and world-historical bursts with irresistible force the framework of merely German or even merely Northern German homeland history and commandingly demands going into the complete process and thus the old Northern German-Scandinavian core region as it lives within us today.

The shortest path to we lead through the entire world. The most thorough introspection occurs after long wandering. World expanse of knowledge and depth of soul, effectiveness toward the outside and introspection within oneself, deed and reflection demand and promote each other.

Homeland becomes what it is through the blood. When first only the Ichthyosaurs and Deinotherium lived in it, it was not yet our homeland, yes, not even our environment. The remains of such creatures, the primitive rock on its bed, are important as local facts, which the class uses practically to broaden the picture of the world. But the concept homeland encompasses more, something different, something more important.

Homeland leads far out into the spiritual. We remember the homeland from which we come and the other one we enter, which we want to win through work on our own soil.

So, homeland means for us representatives of this new desire one foundation of our cultural policy orientation. And an old word offers itself for this orientation itself as well: love (Minne).

Its basic meaning, which stretches back to the Indo-Germanic root, is deep inner self-reflection. A friendly reflection overcoming temporal and spatial distance is meant.

The monuments of prehistory are landmarks for this love for the ancestors. They keep awake the memory of the deeds of the ancestors and heroes and awaken the feeling of obligation toward the future. Since the oldest generations traced themselves to the gods, one drank the love goblet (Minnebecher) at the festival in their memory. The meaning also resulted from the friendly attitude that lies in the word love (Minne): Friendly agreement, kind setting aside of quarrel.

These meanings are far from that eroticism. The word love (Minne) received the connection to the sexual only late and in the Northern German region characteristically not at all. But the connection to the succession of generations, of the unity of soul and blood, clearly dominates.

The world-historical and social scientific view under the sign of the racial and folkish idea and the conclusions from it hence stand for us under the sign of the deepened homeland idea and of love (Minne).

The Nordic Races Struggle in the Meaning of the World

What does this love then to awaken within us? First, it guides our gaze into our own history, then into our prehistory, then into the history of our race. Not only the German Middle Ages, German antiquity and the other Indo-Germanic, northern race folks' step before us, and their struggle as well for the leadership in the culture shaping of humankind is most deeply related to us.

So, our loving, blood-bound, friendly memory, our love, broadens into a worldview and social scientific view. Its object is the Nordic race in the struggle for the meaning of the world.

This struggle plays out today and was yesterday and blazed already in prehistory. One could thus try to proceed from what lies closest to us and trace it back step by step to its origins in the most distant past just to not lose the living connection with the present.

This would mean never really finding it. It can always only be carried out in details; it shrinks with the distance; for in the older times, information becomes ever sparser until it finally runs dry. So, we risk losing under our hands the richness that we want to look at and let glow within us, just like rivers become ever more unassuming the closer they are to their source and disappear in the rocks. In no way does one see the tree better if one looks down from one of its branches along the trunk toward the roots. Rather, one needs a decent interval to gain an overall view, even of the course of the rivers and of the enormous lakes and finally the seas and their steaming toward the sun.

All too many details are the fiercest enemies of any picture, encompassing vast spaces and times. Instead, everything is shortened to the most extreme, so that the overview can first become perceivable, comprehensible, kept and hence, the force of a truthful view can emanate from it.

That here it is about our race, yes, our soul as well, and indeed back then and today still, must result from the overall content and not from artificially produced or preserved connections to our present.

Just like the globe has five continents, so must our world-historical and social scientific view show the Indo-Germanic personalities with their five high cultures in India, Iran, Greece, Italy and of the Germans resting on Germanic foundation. Only the combined view of these various folk personalities and their cultural creations produces the deepened overall picture of the Nordic race, of its inner diversity and of its possibilities.

One must guard against wanting to reduce such personalities, be they individual, important, creative people, be they entire folks, to a simple formula; for behind each stands a plentitude of the whole of life, and especially behind the personality of folks.

Who Goethe, Beethoven or Rembrandt is, one can hardly show from afar, one must absorb their works, and nothing has such an educating effect as this kind of association with leading people.

The same thing is true of the great folks clearly pronounced in their cultural works. What we show about them from here cannot replace the direct contact with them, it can only lead toward them.

Also, each personality is a center point of meaning for all around it. It gives life meaning, and it fights for it. Hence, the development of the five great Indo-Germanic folk personalities in their high cultures is simultaneously the struggle for the meaning of the world.

We stand in the middle of this struggle and yet simultaneously see it from high watch as a process of fate, from which, precisely because we are born into it, we base our inviolate freedom.

Indo-Germanic People

The distribution of the dominant races around the end of the Stone Age corresponded, despite many later displacements and obliterations, basically to the picture that today still shows the racial variants in Europe's population, on the coasts of the Mediterranean Sea and in Asia Minor.

In Europe's north, in southern Scandinavia and in Northern Germany, we have before us the core region of the Nordic race and of the masculine race closely related to it. From the east, the Alpine race is just like a wedge deep into Europe. The Dinaric race stretches from the Pyrenees through the Alps and Balkans, and the

Near Eastern race, probably originally closely related to it, through Asia Minor and the Caucasus. Behind this wall, which in earlier times was in front of the great mountain chain and was then pushed away under the pressure from the north, lie in the west around the Mediterranean Sea the folks of the Mediterranean race, in the orient the folks of oriental (Semitic) race closely related to them.

European peasant cultures, into which the Late Stone Age in Europe flowed, are already involved in the tense relationships between the Nordic (and masculine), the Alpine, Dinaric and Mediterranean races. But the old High Cultures lie in the orient. In Mesopotamia, on the Nile, on the Indus, the peasant settlement around the city's castle was expanded already in the early historical period, that means in part even before the fourth millennium B.C., and a cultural movement of urbanization emanates from here which slowly but steadily over millennia spreads through the Mediterranean lands to the distant west and even more slowly toward the north, only that the North resists it the most stubborn, and up to the beginning of the German Middle Ages successfully.

The plough culture, the steer as work animal, the milk economy and the related customs, the foundations of the peasantry, however, despite their great age and their rich development in the orient, must not have their origin there, they can also already have it in the European north. The oldest plough comes from the fourth millennium B.C. and was found in Eastern Frisia.

Seats & Wanderings of the Indo-Germanic Folks
(According to Bruno R. Schultz)
Border of the Kentom & Sateni Folks

Europe's Late Stone Age peasant cultures and the orient's urban cultures show clear signs of torpidity when the Indo-Germanic folks, coming from Europe's north, themselves grown upon peasant foundation, spread over them, advance on daring treks into the deepest southeast and complete their world-historical foundations.

The Indians and the Iranians (Persians and related ethnic groups), the Scythians in southern Russia. And later the Prussians, Latvians, Slavs belong to the eastern branch of a great family of folks whose western branch is formed by the Greeks, Thracians and

Phryger, Italians Celts, Illyrians, and Germanic folks. One classifies all them together according to both their must distantly separate representatives, the Indians and Germanic people, by the artificial name coined merely from the language tree of Indo-Germanic.

But not only by language, rather also by race, they originally formed a unity. The oldest testaments of the individual folks, even in the new residences, always show basically the same racial traits, at least for the upper stratum. They are the traits of the Nordic race. The ideal of beauty of the oldest poets of these folks agrees, and the artists portray it in their pictorial works even into the later period.

India, Iran, Armenia, Asia Minor, Greece, Italy, Spain, Britain, however, were first conquered by these folks. The Italians came from beyond the Alps, the Greeks as well from the north, the Phryger from beyond the Bosphorus, to their later residences. Still in Herodot's time, in Russia, merely the west and the south belonged to the Scythians. The treks of these folks show predominantly a spread from north toward south, from northwest toward southeast.

The older, still continuous settlement region before the swarming out of the individual folks, we hence imagine along a central line from the Baltic to the Black Sea. The name Nordic race is hence already sufficiently justified from this, since the core folk of Indo-Germanic man, which embodies this race the purest, yes, almost only, and already possesses a significant, firmly solidified culture, according to these facts must have stemmed from Europe's north. During their spread, however, these folks absorb into their development other, old indigenous population, presumably racially and linguistically in part more diverse than themselves, permeate them or subjugate them as well. That is the chief impulse for the formation of the individual Indo-Germanic folks.

Already early, these folks fell into two groups, and indeed according to language and culture.

In the northwest group, *"hundred"* is *"kentom"* and *"horse"* is *"ekwos"*, in the southeast group these words are satem and as was, so a palatial plosive (k) has regularly become a palatial sibilant (s). The southeast group is the younger one. The folks in the northwest group are more settled peasants, those in the southeast group on the open steppe in part wandering herdsmen and horsemen. The split into both these groups presumably resulted, because the eastern one, the more it pushed into the Eastern European low plain and the facts of this world, pushed steppe into an independent development.

Initially, the main weight lies not with the eastern, linguistically as well younger group, rather with the western one, which settles accounts with the already decayed cultures of other Late Stone Age peasant folks and awakens new life from their legacy, to then, as various individual folks, the Italians, Greeks, Thracians, Phyrger, in part also Illyrians, penetrate deeper into the south and southeast.

The role of the south-eastern Germanic people is corresponding and world-historically just as significant. As Indians, Iranians, Kimmerier, Scythians, they break into the super-annulated urban cultures of the southeast and of the old orient and reshape them into a new one, pulsating with their new will.

What comes to us and the into the entire world from the later impulses of antiquity, of the orient as well, has all passed through the reshaping and purifying spirit of these Italians, Greeks, Iranians, Indians and whatever they are all named, and both branches of the Indo-Germanic folks, the eastern and the western, have in the same way had a world-historical and social scientifically decisive share in the culture shaping of humankind. Even if the Nordic race is not the creator of *"all"* culture, everything that surrounds us today as culture has become what it is only through the deepening intervention of the Nordic race and of the Indo-Germanic folks determined by it.

The swarming out of the Indo-Germanic folks did not exhaust the Nordic race. Rather, it immediately planted a new seed leaf. While the Indo-Germanic land acquisition in the expanses of the south and southwest was still in full swing, the internally totally independent Germanic nationality formed in the old ancestral land of the Nordic race, in the present-day Lower German region, around 1,800 B.C., between the Illyrians in the east and southeast and the Celts in the southwest and west. It remained the solid support of the Nordic race in its ancestral regions.

Surrounded by other tribe related folks like the Illyrians and Celts, they were initially for millennia not directly involved in the mighty history of the south and southeast and could substantially develop their kind through their own energy and maintain it in great unity, until they, too, under the pressure of worsening climate, which at the end of the Bronze Age made the north inhospitable, took land in the east up to the Black Sea, won territory against the Celts in the west and south, and finally, around the end of their second millennium, through contact and fighting with the Romans become entangled in southern cultural events. The folk wandering and Viking Age, both the peak events of the third and final Germanic millennium, and the flowing of a Germanic kingdom into German kingdom, were the result.

The world historical significance of these events is determined according to the gain they have brought and how much of it has or should have an effect still today in the cultures of the leading folks, if currents and forces had not inferred that were opposed to the Nordic race and its desire for the ultimate and unconditional, (forces) which wanted to destroy the freedom of the spirit that follows from its truthfulness, and establish their own power instead. The legacy of humankind in its great cultures is simultaneously a struggle for this legacy itself, a competition of what has been found, but often also a losing or even annihilating of legacy values. Attacks seldom succeed completely.

Great deeds, especially in the mind, continue to have an effect and can be deduced from the traces they leave behind. Then our own essence speaks to us again, warns and enlightens us and helps us in our own distress. It combines with all well-preserved knowledge and shows us our path.

Only in this sense can world history be practiced successfully as the history of ideas. It was also a valuation and will always remain such, but it depends on who values. Is it the ones who are biased in their intentions, who fear the truth, if it contradicts these intentions, or is it the ones who can stand above it?

The struggle of the races, folks and cultures is continued in the spiritual with intellectualized means, and the decisions that are made here are no less grave.

The North & the Old Orient

The great opposites are the Indo-Germanic north and the pre-Indo-Germanic, old orient. They show up more distinctly in the spiritual, in the religious.

Indo-Germanic religiosity is in its beginnings different from everything that we know from Jewry, Christianity, Buddhism, Islam, yes, even from the Mazdah doctrine of Zarathustra.

One can distinguish two large groups: Moses, Jesus, Buddha, Mohammed, Zarathustra and religion founders and saviors. Even Jewry already knows the Messiah; that is the younger group.

To the older one belongs to Jaho as city god of Jerusalem and the Roman-Greek religion with its city divinities, as they were in vogue in the orient's old urban culture until the Sumerians and Akkader.

The Indo-Germanic culture, and hence also religion, is originally non-urban. The shrines lie far from the settlements, and one has the greatest one as hearth in one's own home; even in the later period, the festivals are still rural.

The Indo-Germanic religion has as a core the reverent attitude toward the eternally transmutable powers in effect in the universe, which, especially as heavenly light beings, are thought of as being of most general, supra-personal and almost impersonal kind. Fate is considered the larger or smaller share of man in this light world, which is determined by him through birth.

Light, right, order and the course of the world are based on each other.

For right rests on insight, this on enlightenment about one's own inner light share. Right creates order among people, like the divine light powers regulate the course of the world, so that an order corresponds to the other or should correspond, after all.

The worship of the ancestors depends on this light religion, on the presumption of divine descent of one's own family. Earthly existence is only a segment of the great connection. The dead are forces at work in the universe, just like the living. One believes that the enlightened, until their measure is full, or their hour calls them, live in the domain of heaven, or also that they regulate the fertility of the field meadow, themselves enter the meadow, into plants and animals, and are attested in the bodies of human beings as a part of new life in that people consume the sacrificial animal or hunted animal or - in the later stage of field cultivation - the harvest yield.

Hand in hand with such doctrines, under the progressing renunciation of the supra-personal, impersonal, almost physical aspect of them, the powers are reinterpreted into personal divinities who administer specific sphere of life or of nature and, invoked through prayer or sacrifice, help human beings. But according to name and significance, the sky god goes back into the Indo-Germanic primeval period, whom the Greeks name Zeus, the Indians Djaus, the Romans Ju-piter (that means Ju - father) and the Germanic people Tiwaz (Nordic Tyr, German Ziu).

The term *"god"* is still rooted in the impersonal stage. It means *"the called one"*, whereby the wish of the calling, praying, sacrificing human being, but also the power, can be meant, in which the possibility of the fulfilment of the wish is included.

One strives, perhaps already according to foreign examples, through symbolic actions, for example, in dance, to imitate the effectiveness of the powers and gain influence over them and direct them according to wish. It is less magic than an escalated form of prayer. A strong spiritual-moral direction limited the arbitrariness in the establishment of the connections, of the symbolic similarities. One does not so much follow obvious harmonies, rather one aims for ordered, founded connections. Certain functions, for example, braiding and weaving, serve the purpose of protecting oneself against the inclemency of weather, but also other attack. Something similar is true for squaring with the axe, hammering, defense with the sword, with the lance, etc.

Therefore, among Germanic people, the powers are still called late, yet totally in the sense of the impersonal level, Hafte (fastener) and Bande (bond) in the literature of the scalds, and the *"conjurer"* can himself exert power through stitching and binding; or, on the personal level, the gods get tools as symbols of their power, or the goddesses of fate braid, spin and weave.

The religion of the pre-Indo-Germanic orient is totally different. It comes to light complete already in the documents of the Sumerian time, and despite the great spatial and time stretch of the old orient, it has changed little.

In the city stands the house of the god, who is physically portrayed by the picture of the gods. The king and priest serve him. One feeds him and gives him women. His power reaches as far as the city. If the city was defeated, then one led the god away in chains, just like the ruler. The gods were also sent on visits to each other, subjugated gods housed in the side rooms of the temple. Since the chief god sought world importance, the belief in a single god grew from this. Even the intellectualized god of the Jews is totally bound to his city and his temple.

The will of God or of the gods is inscrutable, man ignorant and by nature sinful and exposed to attacks by demons. Sin is something like impurity and being free of it hence has little to do with mortality, and this kind of purity is also little to do with cleanliness. The priests prescribe what one may eat, what is pure, pleasing to God. They try to figure out God's will form omens and heavenly manifestations and to guide it through acts of magic and sacrifices. They determine the measures for time, space, weight to regulate the taxes of the subjects here below according to heavenly processes, and a caricature of the science of heavenly processes emerges, astrology.

Prophecy and magic prove that one could not extract a cause from the river of events and delineate its effect. Instead of searching for the cause, one proceeded from something conspicuous and compared the next conspicuous thing, not the effect. So, one established arbitrary connection between such conspicuous events and fell into a kind of relationship delusion.

The practical application of such false orientation, likewise the corresponding technology, although admittedly a meaningless one, is magic. The magician squeezes water out of a sponge while he beats on a cymbal and imagines that he can produce rain and thunder. Or he makes a doll of his enemy and expects this person will go blind if it pokes out its eyes. Both times, the connection lies in an arbitrarily established similarity.

Only in beginnings do the efforts to relate the heavenly to the earthly reach into law. The divinity indeed hands King Hamurapi the law scroll, but in these stands neither that misdeed angers god nor that it provokes divine wrath. Treaties with other folks are sworn by the gods on both sides. The others are entangled in the net of gods alien to them, who strike down the one who breaks the treaty. Law has as a purpose the calm and satisfaction of the subjects, the king's fame after death. The goal of all wishes is life, more life. For death is near and destroys all joys. The dead reside in a dark place, the grave, where rainwater is their drink, clay their food.

The Indians & Iranians

The Indians first separate from the eastern group of the Indo-Germanic people, if one disregards presently still difficult to determine older strains in the Hittite Empire and elsewhere in the old orient, and one of their tribes, the Hari (the Blondes), appears around 1,400 B.C. as an ally of the Hittites. But their contact with the old orient was not lasting. Their main mass will have reached Afghanistan and the Hamun-see around 1,000 B.C., and from there, they conquered the land of the five rivers.

Meanwhile, around 1,000, the first Iranians immigrate, bring down the empire of the Near Eastern Chaldean on Wannsee and gradually establish themselves in the whole of the Zagros Mountain range. They are the Mede and the Persians. A major group of the Mede units into larger states, while the Persians still sit 830 kilometers north of the Mede and only at the beginning of the 6th century arrive in Persis.

The highland of Iran, just made a new homeland through the land acquisition, immediately proves itself a reliable base from which an extensive, daring foundation follows: the world empire of the Persian King Kurusch (Kyros). It stretches already around 538 from India to Egypt and Greece; Kambudschija II. (Kambyses) even conquers Egypt temporarily. Upon his death, a rebellion breaks out in the empire, but the great Darejawosch (Darius I) can quickly beat it down (519, inscription of Bagistan). The new state is secure for a long time.

Behind the rushing external events that lead to this result stands as driving force the inner opposition and fresh employment of Nordic folks against the inhabitants of the land and their super-annulated culture.

The Iranians, like the Indians, are not merely horsemen, rather simultaneously also peasant warriors, who set off with all their mobile belongings for land acquisition, but they know neither cities nor royal palaces nor images of divinities and intricate cults nor writing and everything that relates to it. The folks of the old orient have all possessed these institutions for millennia. The king, the priests, warriors, officials, traders, usurers degraded the citizens of the city to servile subjects, the peasants on the land to statute-laborers.

The cultures of the orient in the ancestral region have long fossilized into civilization and decayed, while the movement of urbanization that once emanated from this ancestral region has slowly but steadily spread for a good two millennia already toward the distant west and even more slowly toward the north. In Italy, the cities are just now sprouting up, when the Italians who arrived recently also already grow into them, the still blossom in the Aegean circle when the Greeks take them over, in the old orient they have already become old, when the Iranians breathe new life into them.

But in all three regions, the conquerors encounter essentially fare incomparably mightier, the Iranian or even the Indian advance distances itself incomparably farther from the ancestral regions, the internal distance of the peasant-warrior culture of the Iranians from the, despite all signs of decay, mighty urban culture of the old orient is huge. Rome could not by a long shot be something so new, so strange for Germanic people as Susa or even Babel for the Persians. For Rome had already grown from Italian-lndo-Germanic spirit and despite everything that divided them related to nature, while in the old orient Indo-Germanic nationality had never established itself anywhere before the Iranian land acquisition and empire foundation.

And one could more readily compare the Spaniards who burst into old America. But what a difference! Those zealots of a darkened Christianity do not let themselves be touched by the radiance and greatness of the old American cultures and destroy them in gold greedy rage, while the Iranians spare the alien folks understanding^ and integrate them as bearers of their empire into their dominating desire.

The Name Aryan

Common to Indians and Iranians is the name Aryan. That is what the old warrior nobility called itself, and it means roughly *"those bound through blood friendship, related"*, and indeed in contrast to the ancient population viewed as racially inferior.

The Indians speak expressly of the light, *"Aryan color"* and contrast it with the dark color of the flat noses whom they found already in the land.

The Iranians tie *"Aryan"* to noble descent. The name Iran comes from the form of Eran of Aryan, and that means *"Aryan land"*.

The great Persian King Darejawosch calls himself *"Aryan of Aryan seed"*. The pictorial works that portray him, his relatives and followers show Persians, Mede, and Scythians as people of Nordic race.

The term Aryan also applies to the Mede and probably to the Scythians related to them, yes, it passes along to their successors, the Alans, whose name likewise developed phonetically along a different path from Arjan, finally to the Oseten, pushed off to the Caucasus, continuing with the Alan, who still today call themselves Iron, that means Iranians.

Since olden times, one also forms individual names, in whose first part one refers to the Aryandom of the bearer, for example Arjaramna (grandfather of Darejawowsch) or Arjapeithes (King of the Scythians, mentioned by Hereodotos).

According to Greek accounts, a son of Darejawosch is supposed to have been named Arjamenes, which sounds quite close to the old honourable god Arjaman shared by Iranians and Indians, who characteristically was originally the god of marriage. In India, one also designates with Arjaman the bridegroom, in Iran the clansmen, too. Besides that, the god was healing, priestly physician, among the Indians still in a later time as ringleader of the ancestors, and the songs of the Rigweda already move his path to heaven. All these interpretations are internally connected. Down here, the bridegroom corresponds to the god of marriage, who as clansman takes care of the continued existence of his clan. Through this, death is conquered, like how a physician through healing saves the sick person from death. But all that is already presupposed in the divine's form is ancestral father, back to whom the clan of human beings trace themselves, and who as they first travelled the path of the world of the living into eternity.

So, one derives the succession of noble generations from the heavenly world of light. In this sense, Darejawosch as well designates himself as *"Aryan from Aryan seed"*. For his word for seed means spark of light. According to the general Aryan view, the seed is a fluid form of the heavenly fire. Such ideas were so powerful that even many centuries later they radiated from the Arian and Iranian, influenced east to the tribe related folks, to Celts and Germanic people. For the Germanic people, the name Ariowistus proves this, that means *"from Aryan seed"*, which the ruler of the Sweben bears who fights with Caesar, and the name of the Goth Arjobindus, that means *"Aryan allied"*, in the 5th century A.D.

Both names are in the second part Germanic and so formed that they attest to full understanding for the first part as well. Finally, the expression *"the most Aryan of the heirs"* appears on the rune stone of Tune in Vingulmörk in south-eastern Norway on the Swedish border in the 6th century A.D. Then, a millennium and a half later, the folkish movement in Germany takes up the term Aryan from the Indians. A fundamental clarification of northern racial consciousness and the delineation against everything unconditionally alien, especially Jewry, was the result.

The Commandments of Aryan Law

Common to Indian and Iranians is furthermore the concept of order. The word for it, Artam, among both folks means course of the world, world-order, truth, right? Something similar is the fas of the Roman, the Themis or Heimarmene of the Greeks, the Saelde of the Germanic people. The order of the Artam encompasses the heavenly world of light and the generations of human beings who trace themselves from it and the whole of nature. Even the gods are only a part of it. Piety means agreeing with it. The faith already lies in the word Aryan, and like with this one, so does one also tend to individual names with Artam, for example Artaphemes (*"through truth radiating"*), Artachschaffa (distorted by the Greeks into Artaxerxes; *"through truth ruling"*). Images of God are originally alien to this view. Marriage and clan constitution, right and cult refer to the sacrifice of the hearth. Livestock and plants, receiving and giving, take part in the meal where they are cooked.

According to old Indian custom, the father of the house makes a daily fourfold sacrifice into the hearth fire: to the gods, the ancestors (parents), the heroes (from whose worship the concept of the fatherland evolved), the guests. These sacrifices correspond to the same number of commandments of divine law. The Persians detest their violation as ingratitude and root of all bad. In the old Indian law book of Manus, five commandments of human law are added to this: purity, control over the senses, abstinence from harming creatures, abstinence from unlawful acquisition, truthfulness. In Greco-Roman law, the three vengeance demanding misdeeds that provoke the instigation of conflict correspond to the three middle commandments. They are murder, rape, theft. So, the nine commandments of old Aryan law result:

1. Honor the gods
2. Honor the parents
3. Honor the heroes (The Fathers, the Fatherland)
4. Honor guests
5. Commandment of purity
6. Ban on murder
7. Ban on rape
8. Ban on theft
9. Commandment of truthfulness (Loyalty)

The ten commandments of the Bible (Exodus XX) are accordingly derived from an older path still to be more closely proven, and hence, if one looks closer, there are also only the following nine:

1. You shall have no other gods.
2. You shall make no idols.
3. You shall not take the name of Jehovah frivolously.
4. Remember to honor the Sabbath.
5. Honor father and mother.
6. You shall not kill.
7. You shall not commit adultery (Covet your neighbor's wife).
8. You shall not steal (not covert your neighbor's house).
9. You shall not bear false witness.

The last four commandments fit well in both series. The fifth commandment of the Bible (according to the above listing, not according to the catechism) goes: Honor father and mother, so that you live long in the land that Jehovah, your god, has given to you as your own. It hence corresponds to the second Aryan commandment (honoring of the ancestors), and the basis for the third Aryan commandment; for the fatherland is replaced by the promised land. The fourth and fifth Aryan commandments have been pushed out by the Sabbath, and the first Aryan commandment has expanded into three in the Bible. The zeal for monotheism has destroyed the balance, while the nine statutes of Aryan law are structured, clear and firm.

Aryan law rests on the clan, at whose head the father of the house stands, Sumerian-Semite law on the rule of the Priest-King, who stands under protecting the city divinity. While according to the Sumerian-Semite view the state prosecutes and punishes law violation, according to the Aryan view, the wronged party may gain justice himself, and the court merely decides what is right, if the case is in dispute, without carrying out the verdict.

Aryan law punishes only the evil intent (dolus), Sumerian-Semitic law is only the success. Also, with bodily injury and similarly in other cases, the Aryan seeks to eliminate the hostility through reconciliation, while the Sumerian and Semite demand an eye for an eye, a tooth for tooth. Every limb of the perpetrator should be punished, which he has harmed on the injured party, while the Aryan punishes the one that has offended.

But all that is not merely racially determined bearing, it is also already in many things' conscious world-view orientation. And it clearly pushes for comprehensive religious shaping that has prevailed most splendidly in India, but already deviating from the Aryan basis, in creating the Buddha, in Iran, consciously reaching back to the Aryan orientation bearing (Gesinnungshaltung), in the religion of Zarathustra.

The Indians

The Indo-Germanic folk advancing the farthest toward the southeast, the Indians, have it the hardest, preserving its unique nature. Only little fresh blood flows to it from its ancestral regions over the course of its history. The climate is murderous for the Nordic race and a numerically vastly superior, older native population has already achieved a substantial level of urban culture in the Indus region and even possesses its own pictorial alphabet when the Indian tribes invade. Outer and inner history of the Indians is hence a moving spectacle. The Aryan energy is so great, the old native population so diverse, that a cleavage of dispositions opens before us that stretches far into the intellectual, which escalates to insanity and has its equal nowhere else.

The oldest document of the Indians, the Rigveda, a collection of songs to the gods, still stands on the Aryan level and contains isolated memories of a trek, but nothing of the pre-Indian, very noteworthy urban culture of the land, which is well known to us through excavations (for example, in Mohenjo Daro); just like the oldest Germanic poetry also relates nothing of Rome or Byzantine. Alien also penetrates already occasionally into the oldest Indian world of the gods and into the orientation with which it is cherished, and this escalates in the priestly texts (the Brahmanas), the philosophical literature (the Upanishad), the heroic epics (the Mahabharata and the Ramayana).

The strangest is the inclination to withdrawal from the world, but at first it does not yet have a downright destructive effect. If the Aryan Indian had fulfilled his duties toward life, then in his old age he could devote himself to reflection about world and man. One found back then, for the first time, thoughts full of depth and sublimity, such as were thought again by our great philosophers only much later. Indian tradition characteristically ascribes them to members of the warrior nobility, and the priests come to them for dialog and let themselves be taught.

But then a priesthood trapped in alien thought gains power over king and Aryan warrior-nobility, claims the noblest blood, allows the Aryan importance only in second place, and on this false foundation seeks to combat race-mixing through a law that comes much too late and can create, instead of a structuring according to blood purity or professions, merely a quite arbitrary division according to rigid castes. One replaces the race idea, which rests on the knowledge of heredity, with the doctrine of reincarnation; according to it the Pariah as well and even any animals can hope, through services whose moral value often seems questionable, to be reborn into the highest castes.

It thus undermined the meaning of the nobility, political will paralyzed and empire foundations beyond India do not take place. Intellectual processes correspond to the political ones. The energy of philosophical thought, which had sought to overcome death through knowledge or fathom the origins of the world from the secrets of one's own soul, soon runs dry. One does not clearly grasp the connection between cause and effect and tracks it out of religious fear, not for its own sake. Hence, the Indians remain denied their own natural science.

External magic delusion and shocking superstition break in. The dispositions tom back and forth between wishes and fears accept connections, which they manufacture themselves, to be true and misunderstand the force of genuine knowledge so much that they trust in the power of these caricatures to intervene causally into reality and change its track. Yes, one becomes fixated in some crazy-sublime idea to the point of asceticism, thinks up corresponding long-term body positions that cause ecstatic conditions or surrenders oneself to horrible penitence exercises to gain superhuman strength or to free oneself from this valley of woe.

One ascribes universal power to the sacrifice, but only if an exaggerated, hair-splitting ritual is fulfilled. The Aryan idea of Artam, the sacred legal order, is interpreted as sacrifice arrangement, the sacrifice and the sacrifice site referenced to the creation of the world, the world regions, the gods as protectors of these world regions, and to their sacred animals, and the priests base their rule on this extravagant symbolism, which they pass off as their secret.

The heavenly fire, from which the Aryan traces their generations, is reinterpreted into the consuming sexual desire of desires and passions. Already earthly life is viewed as hell, the body as a cage. One sees a pitilessly rolling wheel in birth and death. Will and deed drive it onward. To come to rest, one must stop these drives. The hero's grave in the house at the crossing of two main roads, reshaped into Stupa, into walled relic shrine amidst splendid grounds, now holds the physical remains of a savior, of Buddha, whose doctrine is based on total coming to rest and hence on nothingness: a rejection of the world full of sublimity and yet a refuge from it out of the inability to master it. And only as this rejection of oneself has Aryan thought as the doctrine of Buddha, far behind India's Aryan part and especially outside of India, got the importance of a world religion of the folks of the Far East. With its organized priesthood, its cloisters, its monks, and nuns, it counts there today perhaps more followers than Christianity.

The significance of Buddhism for us, however, lies not only in that it could stimulate the attention of such a clear and deep thinker as Schopenhauer or finds resonance circles, rather because it is a model's wrong path. The demand to cease procreation so that the wheel stands still, the flame dies, despite everything appeals to influential forces of intellect and soul, hence precisely exterminates the people who are capable of this soaring and destroys the soil from which it has itself grown.

Iran

The Iranians stand closer to us than the Indians.

Indian literature is plentiful, Iranian almost lost because of the storms that have swept across the land. But the remnants and surrounding after-effects attest to the old greatness.

Four things especially move us:

- First, the old Persian kingship and energy how a new one forms after Alexander's invasion, which brings the old traditions to fresh blossoming.

- Second, the deep bond of the Iranian with nature, which escalates to conscience care for race and to religious emotion for it.

- Third, Zarathustra's religion, in which, for the first time in humankind's history of ideas, moral doctrine and religion become a unity.

- Fourth, the effect of this creation and of Iranian spirit on the surrounding folks, which in various indirect waves also reaches deeply into our German spiritual life.

Indian history is not world history; Iranian is that like hardly another and far more so than Greek.

Iran's political history, beyond its political content, has a spiritual one that the Greek does not have; for in it, with Zarathustra's doctrine, it is simultaneously a struggle by king, warrior-nobility, and peasantry against a power-hungry, idol-serving priesthood.

The Persians developed a government that Greece does not know: its kings give lands and folks as fiefdoms.

Seen from Persepolis, the Greeks' Persian wars are periphery events. We know them only in Greek portrayal, and that is not better than the World War in the portrayal by the enemy press.

The cry *"They are barbarians!"* Echoed already back then. But the Greeks do not overthrow the great Persian Empire, rather the Macedonian overpowers them and Persia and even more.

But Alexander's founding has no permanence. It collapses, and Iran gains strength on its ruins, first in the Parthian Empire (250 B.C.), then in the empire of the Sassanids (226 A.D.), which only cannot invade the invasion by the Arabs. These empires withstood the Romans and provided relief for Germanic man, fended off the Turks and fought against Byzantine, and Iran's new radiance was shared with the surrounding folks, up to China and the Finns and along different paths even up into the German Middle Ages.

Iranian spiritual bearing (Geisteshaltung) is the prerequisite for Iranian religious life, which has found its expression in the religion of Zarathustra. Cattle as helper of the peasant with plowing is something sacred, like the cow as donor of milk, the horse as a riding animal of the warrior, the dog and rooster as guardians of the house; even the cat has a right to a share in the milk as reward to the mice that it devours. The Iranian is grateful to his animals.

The relationship with plants is no less passionate. The king and his distinguished men competed in creating glorious gardens, in which they grew beautiful and fruitful plants and kept noble animals. They turned Persia, which today is largely a salt desert, into a blossoming region. The aromatic rose, the precious peach, that means the *"Persian apple"*, attests to their skill.

According to Iranian-Zarathustrianism view, good is the earth which bears fruit, the water that makes the plants thrive, the fire that bums in the house and cooks the nourishment, and all animals that are helpful for man.

The breeding experience with plants and animals one also applies to man, who takes himself under control. Valued are tall stature, strength, beauty, and all spiritual virtue. They praised women who have the most beautiful body for procreation, who are the most capable of the household. Head of the house asks for light-eyed, intelligent offspring, who are supposed to promote him, house and community, province and land, and the land's glory. The married man has priority over the non-married, the man with many children over the childless man.

The offspring are heavenly fire realized from the seed and hence bearers of faith, whose content comprises the bond with all light. Peasant sense of reality and warrior peasant thought unite here into a highly intellectualized doctrine.

The world of faith in the good creation, to which well-mannered animals and plants also belong, is opposed by the dark, non-spiritual counter-creation of the evil one, the one: pure, victorious truth, the other: the diabolical scheme of insubordinate lie.

Ants and snakes, wolves and other predators all have poisons, belong to this counter-creation, and it is a service to exterminate them.

The hero who kills the dragon becomes the culture-bringer for the Iranian, who clears the thicket, drains the swamps and cultivates the field, or the knight without fear or reproach, who protects the land and his faith against the enemy army, or the wrestling human being, who in the struggle of opposing feelings holds to the good, all of them already bearers of the same spiritual-moral decision, which will take place overall at the end of things, when the god of truth along with the noblest knights take the field against the demon of lie and his spawn and defeat him in order to found his eternal empire.

Three waves have transmitted Iranian spirit to us Germans, each time in odd form. The first two, facilitated through Christianity, are the most important, but the third, which reached us through the advance of the Arabs, who were Iranian influenced in many things, to Spain and through the penetration of the Vikings and crusaders into the orient, is almost just as significant.

The first brought us the Old Testament of the Jews. The Jews in Babylon stood under Persian rule and brought their holy scripture from there to Palestine. Much over one admits, and most of what appeal to us, they owe to the Persians.

The second wave brought us the New Testament, Christianity. The gospels contain much that is Iranian, and to explain that would mean that one explains the Aryan, the Nordic in them. That is a task for the German future and the path that German spirit finds for its inner rest.

The third wave brought us knighthood, love and mysticism, a new form of warrior life bearing, with a new trait of inclination to the eternal.

Greece

More familiar to us than Iran is Greece.

The glory of the Greeks is so great, their achievement in the pictorial arts, literature, history writing, science, life wisdom, are so well known, their culture has through humanism so very much served the leading men of our folk as example for soon half a millennium, and it is also so rich that it is neither possible nor necessary to go into detail.

The Greeks did not distance themselves from the enclosed settlement region of the Nordic folks as far as the Indians; they did not spread a thin ruling stratum over the folks of old high cultures as the Iranians. They took possession of a land of special favor, and they also encountered a naïve population that stood not all too distant from them.

They already brought alone valuable culture goods from the Nordic homeland. For example, the rectangular house with the protruding roof supported by posts, the Magaron House, which, in stone, they transformed into the temple.

Their art embodies in many of their best works the Nordic race's ideal of beauty. For them, beauty expresses physical and spiritual nobility, which keep each other in balance. Their literature, on the old level, deals with fate from a heroic life orientation and peaks in the drama's creation.

The relentlessness of the characters and the logic of the action grip even the historian. Motive and result, cause and effect are pondered and delineated.

In natural science, important laws of nature are the result. Yes, the ideal of causality in nature reveals itself to the Greek researchers: Aristarch of Samos grasped even the movement of the earth around the sun.

The Greeks erect the proud structure of mathematics and of logic exemplary and almost conclusively.

Their thinkers delve into the ultimate questions, and only the descendants of the Germanic people continue this legacy and increase it.

Their physicians create scientific medicine and apply it according to moral principles.

Admittedly, despite strong religious energy, Greece does not produce a religion forcing the world around it into its orbit, but it produces the bloom of philosophy, trust in eternal knowledge and conscientiousness in the world's knowledge.

A good share of Nordic feeling, which keeps distance and is averse to exaggerations, expresses itself in it, and in that the priesthood remains within moderate boundaries and Greek intellect unconditionally free.

It does not always remain true to itself. Two dangers threaten it: the Mediterranean tendency toward pose and the Near Eastern one toward pettifogging. Both enter ruinous mixture in the speaker and sophist, who under the pretext of turning the weaker thing into the stronger one, bends right and, in that he gives himself the appearance of professional expertise, crowds out the experts.

Political division grows, the tribal feuds consume the best blood, offspring are limited, the racially alien lower stratum ascends.

Great artists, researchers, thinkers become ever rarer, and when Greece loses its independence to Rome, the Roman indeed imitates the Greek of the old time, but the Greek of this late time, the Graeculus (Little Greek), the bastards acting Greek, is his slave, toady, buffoon.

Rome

Along with the Greeks, inclination, struggle tie us to the Romans.

The Italians already bring along into their land the germ of the future greatness, the fortified arrangement of their settlement, which is the image of the Roman military camp. But already early, much that is racially alien, from the Etruscans stemming from Asia Minor, flows into the state system, which under them rises to dominance, flows into what is Roman. This shows itself most clearly in its institution of foreseeing the future through superstitious means like reading entrails or reconciling with the angry powers through sacrifice in the event of lighting, miscarriage, and other frightening signs.

There unity in the Roman nature for sobriety escalated sense of reality, high mental energy in the service of an insatiable will for power, a basic tone of the dark and superstitious, strong religious bond. Lacking is the ultimate soaring toward the eternal, artistic transfiguration, the urge for knowledge aimed at the unconditional, at the universally valid. The influence of Greek settlements in Lower Italy creates no sufficient counterweight.

Rome destroys Carthage and saves the folks of the Mediterranean from the Semites, but because it develops from a city state of world power, it only represents its interests, no ideals.

Its mightiest creations, its military, and its law, are exemplary, but in both, it distances itself from an old Italian, Indo-Germanic foundation.

The army, originally the armed clans, become a strictly organized mercenary troop, in its mass foreign to the land, to which the state, when its own blood stream runs dry, sees itself delivered.

Law rests on the family in its relationship to clan and folk. But the family is replaced by the law-bearer, the family father, with unlimited power over his own, even his household members, and the folk tied by blood is replaced by the state, whose citizens finally even freed slaves and bastards from the conquered provinces become. Legal claims based on written law are valid and not eternal law, and the law of the Romans becomes the law for all. Folk law becomes state law, and indeed in a state that falls to pieces.

The northern racial Italians no longer have an advantage over the cunningly naturalized oriental: racial aliens win the highest offices, foreign cults find acceptance, moral decay spreads, Nordic blood seeps into the brew of folks.

Army and law, development of power and protection of interests, intellectual achievements of world-compelling might be for Rome what their religions were for India and Iran, for Greece its philosophy. Just that the religions are fulfilling content for their followers, but both most intellectual creations of Rome soon just shells without core.

However, even the religious denominations have a similar path behind them, as was especially to be seen in Iran. The original doctrine, religion, and moral doctrine, yes, even the philosophizing, were racially determined; participation in sacrifice was limited to clansmen.

Only later did religion broaden from the community of tribe relatives to the community of those bound to one another through a denomination. This new and so very much more external community then became leading in the state and exemplary for others; like the law, it even became for the others a kind of substitute for blood kinship, which they lacked. So, denomination decided, while the race idea, the bond of blood, receded. The path to the world religions was opened.

When Christianity, nourished from Jewish and Iranian sap, comes to Rome, a new core grows in the empty shell. The Roman-Catholic church, with its clergy organized into the fighting church, continues the religion of the Roman army, with its claim to world importance, the empire's claim to worldly power, with intellectualized, religious means.

The Germanic People

Rome does not master two enemies: the Parthians in the east and the incomparably mightier Germanic people. If one wants to correctly assess them, then one must not put them side by side at the height of their activity, rather Indians, Iranians, Greeks, Italians are comparable to them only at the time before they had stepped upon their path of fate. But if one takes it so, then the Germanic people show themselves equal in value, yes, in many things even superior. This race is the remnant that remained in the north, and while the others won and failed, they grew slowly and constantly from their own strength and without the drive from foreign stimulus.

Germanic self-shaping stretches through three millennia.

Germanic man of the Bronze Age (1800 to 800 B.C.) stands close to the earliest Greek. Both know the chariot, both the decorative spiral of jewelry and weapon. But the Germanic manner of decoration is more internally unified, more inward, nobler. Germanic people practice since olden times the artistic carving of wood and are masters in shipbuilding. Sweden's Bronze Age cliff etchings provide a rich picture of it.

Essentially, two pieces of clothing suffice for the Greek and Germanic man: shirt and overcoat, both not tailored.

Even much later, the Greeks can show nothing like the *"Luren"*, Germanic man's large horns, poured from bronze and encompassing three octaves and over 20 notes. Germanic man shows the beginnings of a kind of cult drama already in the earliest Bronze Age as cliff etchings.

Germanic man's twin gods are saviors and rescuers from mortal danger. The dual kingship of the Vandals linked to them has its counterpart in the Dioscuri and the dual kings of the Spartans. This faith even reaches to Iran and India.

Old Nordic praise of the god Thor (Donar) as vanquisher of monsters and giants coincides with old Indian ones of the god Indra.

The next millennium, the early Iron Age (800 B.C. to 200 A.D.), brings hard tests for Germanic man, but also confirmation.

The north becomes cold; the tribes seek land. But an iron wall of armed folks all around must first be broken through in a difficult struggle. Most important is the conflict with the Celts and then with the Romans in the west, the penetration through the Illyrians and the advance to the Black Sea in the east. From here, the Goth Empire, Germanic man, rolls up the Roman border defense at the end of the millennium.

Rome recognized the greatness of Germanic man, but it did not want to acknowledge it. It considered itself superior, but its civilization was a culture of decay and mere appearance. What it wanted to impose upon Germanic man was not very good.

The Germanic military, organized according to clans, rests on the bonds of blood, on voluntary following and daring action. One did not want to imitate Roman subservience, armament, calculation.

Measure, weight, coin stood in the service of Roman trade sucking dry. Germanic tribes rightly banned the importation of wine, but without success. One did not need horticulture, which the Romans themselves had only recently adopted from Greece and Asia Minor.

Stone construction has suppressed the art of Germanic wood construction for a long time. Roman law existed only for the Romans and was usually distorted into injustice. Nothing is comparable to the atrocities of the circus and the exploitation and degradation of the slaves in Rome. Roman religion was a mixture of disbelief and superstition. Life and deeds contradicted the higher religious values, which one proclaimed in full-sounding principles.

One limited the offspring, the Roman nationality declined.

Those Germanic tribes that slid into this ruin become a warning example for the others. Only after Rome had fallen to Germanic man did its legacy become a threat to him. The third millennium, the late Iron Age (200 to 1,200 A.D.), then runs along two lines. Germanic man, on the dawning foundation of the folk wandering and on the tottering one of the Viking Age, in the exultation of his success's strides toward self-portrayal of his nature with new means of expression, deepened will for form, unerring certainty - and Germanic man loses this security everywhere, succumbs to the form imposed upon him and makes it his own, so that the fossilized foreign civilization becomes culture under his guardianship.

During the folk wandering, Germanic man creates a decorative art, animal ornamentation, a new literary art, the heroic songs; in the Viking Age, he escalates both to works of high personal ambition; songs of praise, prose stories, the beginnings of a reality-based history writing are added.

Both these peaks of self-shaping stand in sharp contrast to two valleys of the receding of this self-shaping on the other line of the course and hence simultaneously the peak of a new foreign shaping; the Carolingian Renaissance of antiquity, which sets in about two centuries after the folk wandering and has as a result that the education of the Middle Ages remains folk alien, Latin; and the Italian Renaissance with its effects toward the north. It sets in about two centuries after the Viking Age, and German education remains folk alien, humanistic. Even the Reformation is not effective.

The forward driving spirit of the Nordic race has, meanwhile in the crusades and voyages of discovery, established contact with the intellectual achievements of other folks and cultures. The natural sciences blossom. And Germanic spirit adds a new fruit in them. The picture of the world becomes broader and clearer than ever before, and to an unexpected degree, the knowledge won steps into the service of life.

What is German?

German development plays a leading role in these processes, which stretch across all following Germanic folks. But it cannot be a uniform one, for between it and what is Germanic lie four decisive cracks.

The first crack emerges in the settlement region. Because of the evacuation of the east, the Slavs invade and occupy all Northern Germany up to the Elbe, Central Germany up to the Saale, Bohemia, Moravia, Austria to the Balkans, the earlier Eastern Goth Empire up to the Black Sea. The later German colonization of the east can reverse only a portion of the loss.

The second crack is regarding the cultural orientation. Celts were overrun, but in Lombardy, in Gaul and in Spain, the Germanic conqueror stratum is too weak, the Celtic-Roman population prevails in language and largely in civilization as well, and this swamps the bordering Germanic regions with influences that hamper strengthening on the foundation of the own nationality. The adoption of Roman law is the most conspicuous sign of this process.

The third crack takes place as society. During the long, fateful treks, folk assembly, army constitution, clan system and the old structure of the folk body decline. The kingship gains power, puts slaves and foreigners over the own folk, degrades it over time to subjects, creates cities and states for itself and rules through its house power and through the opposition of the professions.

The fourth crack occurs in the soul of people; for first Eastern Germanic man adopts Christianity in its Aryan form from Byzantine, and the Goth Wulsila translates the Bible around the middle of the 4th century; but then Western Germanic man and especially the Franks adopt it in its Catholic form from Rome. And immediately, new fraternal feuds ignite from the religion of peace, and one exploits religion as means of power. It takes centuries before it really grows into the German soul, and the question, whether and how a genuine inner unity is possible, is due again and again. The consequences of this discord and the various, never-ending attempts to rally oneself for a cure, to make the folk body as well healthier, to overcome the Roman civilization unbearable for a Germanic man in favor of his own culture, and finally to banish the Slavic threat, then make up the inner and outer history of Germandom.

The cracks heal only superficially. New ones, like the Catholic-Protestant one, are added. Even where Germandom merges itself again in its native property, such as in language, the disgusting swarm of foreign language art expressions remains in honor. Much is added to culture in Germany, even immortal, high culture, and yet losing German essence progresses every farther. Humanism brings the contact with classical antiquity, but it takes en gross and does not yet know how to separate the native from the deviant. Finally, the international Jews raises his head, humanity becomes a caricature of itself, the race comes in danger.

If after this look at the whole of the Germanic-German cultural process one wants to answer the question: What is German? then generalizations cannot suffice such as being German means being truthful, being loyal, doing something for its own sake, and so forth. It is already better, when Friedrich Nietzsche responds to it: Being German means still always developing, still having a future.

Lata, according to the law of what has already existed and what is still in effect at the present, means being German, not yet being finished with those four cracks and several others that have been added in the meantime, bearing this fate, but also again and again drawing new energies from it and developing a unique richness of culture shaping. De lege ferenda (De lege ferenda, when used in context, indicates that the speaker or writer is going to propose an idea that would alter existing law through addition or repeal), according to the law that we want to realize in the future, however, means being German from now on banishing old misfortune and paving the path for a happier, more unified, and hence no less rich German culture.

No previous generation has had at its disposal the insights necessary for recovery like us. The whole of world history presents itself to us anew. All the past becomes, according to Nietzsche's words, a cockcrow of our future.

Conclusions

Our own spiritual location before time and eternity is determined from the view of the world historical and idea historical path of the Nordic race and lies the core of the doctrine and the beginning of all practical applications. Even if we cannot conduct systematic experiences with folks, states, cultures like in physics and chemistry, much that is diverse has taken place in history, which, if one observes it correctly, possesses the value of such experiments.

The Confirmation

The folks of other races have not produced a similar confirmation as the folks of the Nordic race, neither in the past nor in the present.

Perhaps one thinks about the brilliant prospects of the folks of the east. But the Chinese in their harbor cities and in America have for several generations been similarly able to grow into European culture as formerly Indo-Germanic man into the culture of the old orient and of the Mediterranean folks, and yet nothing is to be seen of it that here a new race, called for intellectual-moral leadership, intervenes into world history, while among Indo-Germanic man this immediately became visible.

The Japanese, who today have a tremendous birth-rate and claim half the world, stand on the foundation of European civilization and would be impotent without the weapons that we ourselves have supplied them. Whether they would advance the adopted foreign culture on their own must first be shown. Achievements in science and technology exceeding the borrowed are still lacking.

The bearers of the pre-Indo-Germanic cultures of antiquity could no longer continue their own culture, when Indo-Germanic man came. The other races remained in tow.

The Alpine race has no leading foundations and creations to show, neither in gray prehistory nor in its first advance toward the west nor in the many later destructive invasions by the folks of the east into the cultures of Asia Minor and Europe.

The Dinaric race as well has never stood out on its own, politically, or otherwise. Where are the empires that it founded, cultures to which it gave the stamp? One praises its musical talent. But where these folks still have music of their own old level, it is a swaying around a few protruding notes and far distant from everything that we call music in the higher sense.

The Near Eastern race standing close to the Dinaric, however, has entered the competition of the cultures of the old orient. The empire of the Hittites and the empire of the Mitani, however, already stand under Indo-Germanic influence. One could sooner name the empire of the old Elam. But its difference from the other high cultures of the orient is not kind forming.

These high cultures of the old orient belong, like the Cretan-Mycenaean predominantly, the Egyptian almost totally, in the play area of the Mediterranean race, the old Babylonian in that of the oriental race. The role of the certainly non-Indo-Germanic Sumerians and the possibility of older northern racial cultural impulses remain open.

For Europe's Mediterranean race, these accomplishments, seen from a distance, open possibilities.

One can supplement these world historical observations with further observations of the German folk. For example, Northern Germany has not contributed nearly as much to music as Southern Germany. Or: there is not purely Nordic, rather even relatively Alpine appearing Beethoven is a creator of German music towering over almost all others, the predominantly masculine Hindenburg, the father of the fatherland.

The other races in our folk are hence co-determining and likewise important, and only altogether produce the German nationality. With the Nordic racial core, however, on their own, they could hardly bear a high culture in the long run and lead it forward.

Musical talent alone does not suffice; the overall skill lies in something else.

Alpine industry, masculine steadiness, is also valuable. Yes, they can, as Hindenburg's example shows, be decisive in difficult moments.

The Nordic race gives overall direction, leadership.

The others are important admixtures and counterweights. If Nordic daring threatens to lose itself of adventure, heroic spirit in pugnacity, drive for knowledge in eccentricity.

The Mixture

The world historical confirmation of the Nordic race overall is thus confronted among the other races important for our nationality by a confirmation before German history individually.

The five exceptional cases of Nordic determined culture: India, Iran, Greece, Italy, finally Germany, are to be explained precisely from the mixture. One says that the Nordic race on its own was incapable of these achievements; only the admixture with the other races that it encountered produced the favorable result.

In fact, the admixture runs parallel to the escalation of high culture for a stretch. But precisely, this proves that it is not the cause, for otherwise it must precede the escalation. But it is the opposite: as soon as the admixture has progressed, the culture creation staggers, and amidst advanced admixture it declines.

This leads at least - to the no less false - restriction that only moderate mixing has a culture-creative effect, too far-reaching a culture-destroying one. But it is a just appearance that high culture appears because race-mixing is in process. Instead, the *"culture-creative"* race showed its traits already earlier and purer, even if merely as bud. They lie in the spiritual energy and in the moral basic bearing. Here and there, the beginnings are already distinct: the Nordic Megaron house as a model for the Greek temple, the old Italian fortification of the settlement as a model for the Roman army camp.

It is not race-mixing that puts things into motion, rather the stimulus effect of the new environment, of the land, of the people and their culture. Their wandering put the Indo-Germanic folks to the test. Other folks wander as well, for example Huns, Mongols, Arabs; but they do not prove themselves, or only to a very limited degree. One can destroy cultures one encounters, like the Spaniards in the Central American ones, or one can use them as a drive for the development of one's one. Folks receive the opportunity to show what dwells within them, above all, through a new environment.

It immediately compels a spiritual and moral debate and awakens traits that have previously slumbered. The conquerors must learn much and apply what has been learned, and they reject much as alien to their kind or re-shape it in their sense, and from all this combined their results in their new, their own thing.

The five high cultures of the Indo-Germanic folks have as precondition the cultures of the previous population. Where such stimuli are lacking, as with the Celts, Illyrians, Thracians, Baltic folks, Slavs, high cultures do not set in, despite the mixing with the previous population. The new Indo-Germanic cultures are the response of the racial nature and nationality to the new environment.

The red Chinese primrose blooms red at normal temperature, white at higher temperature. The new characteristic is the response to a new environmental stimulus. Being a red Chinese primrose means acting so.

It is a response in the bodily. Only with greater warmth can this plant display the characteristic that lie within it.

And being Indo-Germanic, northern racial folk means to respond in the psychological as well. It means, in the north taming the steed, engaging in dairy farming, cultivating the fields, creating the Megaron house and so forth, and in the new land it means building the Greek temple, creating a Greek culture. Only in Greece can this folk show what lies within it.

The Indo-Germanic folks manage such things in a few generations.

The achieved high culture then works again on its part as environment. The racial properties of the higher order, which have created the bearers of this high culture, are passed along. This happens in two directions.

One passing along runs to the surrounding folks and especially to the tribe-related, blood-related small farmers in the north, and that is the backflow into the homeland. Legacies of the higher order that flow back to the north in this manner are no longer totally alien to it, they have already passed through tribe-related blood, are hence more easily adopted, but because of much bending of Nordic bearing which they have suffered, they also contain many dangers. The influence of antiquity on Germanic man from antiquity through the Renaissance to humanism is the great example of this process. Germanic man's wanderings eventually meet it half-way. Iran's influence also takes such paths.

The other passing along runs to the later generations of the own folk. But the mixing is already underway and has paralyzed the old energy.

If one notices the consequences, it is usually already too late. The reactions of the initially overcome foreign nature set it, create division, uncertainty, boredom.

Not the advanced mixing first leads to decline, rather already the one began introduces it.

The Failure

The world's historical failure hence accompanied the world historical confirmation of the great Indo-Germanic foundations each time.

One flees from the reality that one can no longer overpower into the intellectual, the original orientation changes into its opposite.

If the Indian warrior nobility wanted to conquer the world through its own heroic action, then the Indian penitent of the late period seeks to overcome *"the world"* through self-destruction - despite all greatness and tragedy, a warning for us, not a model.

The blood-bound, religious worldview and moral doctrine of Iranian man ultimately, in the great world religions that emerge from it, become general religious affirmation, which even the foreigners make - precisely because of the tremendous effect in space and time and inwardly, a warning for us, not an example.

The nobility breeding of northern racial Greek man, based on clan formation, because municipal code in the foreign city produces majority decisions and democracy and runs dry in a general advocate political education - although brought close to us for half a millennium by the humanists, a warning for us, not a model.

In the Roman state, the social structure and law of the Roman folk becomes a foundation alien to it, a complicated system of legal concepts is presented as universally valid and is also imposed on us and crowds out our native law, and throughout a millennium we cannot do enough to expand the alien and lose ourselves in it - a warning for us, not a model.

Full of warnings, finally, is also our own German history. No lesser than Lagarde characterized it as the constantly advancing loss of German essence. But what has played out in the other Indo-Germanic folks have not merely played out around us, rather also for us. Our special case comes into a larger context and becomes comprehensible in its causes, curable in its shortcomings. What the others managed and what befell them serves us as application and teaching.

Everything is also at work to manifold degrees in our German history of ideas, as Roman law, as Christianity and church, as humanism and in many other institutions, to each of which we stand differently, if we accept them as German fate and differently, if we are knowledgeable of the native and the alien in them and allow this knowledge to ripen within us will-forming.

Feebleness & Energy

Because of the cracks in our nationality, of the inhibitions in its development, of the influx of exemplary results, but also the diverting wrong conclusions of tribe-related cultures, emotional remnants have set in inside our own, which must be worked out, inferiority complexes that must be dismantled and overcome through uncovering the creative energies.

Again and again, one has hammered into us that our ancestors were coarse beasts, had nothing from themselves and owed all their education to the foreign property of the far superior east, south and west. One spoke of our' 'inability for form" and praised antiquity, the French or even China, to banish it; one even dared to drivel about an inability for the moral.

The opposite is true.

Old Germanic art in the Bronze Age and again, with different forms, in the animal ornamentation of the folk wandering and Viking Age, had strict style laws, Germanic literature and an incomparably powerful force of fashioning and its own legality. Through the favoring of the foreign forms presented as exemplary, as great, and significant as they are in themselves, the soul is hindered in developing its wings for the flight to the isles of its own yearning. Form becomes prison and chain, if it does not grow from the own, and it is no wonder, if inability arises from a confusion of imposed forms.

In the moral, it is similar.

The so often championed view that before Christianity, genuine morality existed nowhere, aside from perhaps the Jews, is just as outrageous as narrow-minded, and visibly false. One must not simply equate morality and Christianity as one, and there is much high morality outside of Christianity, which in its denominations encompasses only a fraction of humankind, even of cultured humankind.

We will never share the dogmatic intolerance of Catholicism and Protestantism, rather oppose it with evident determination, wherever it is challenged.

What hinges on the moral values of Germanic man shows itself, especially in the north, when Christianity destroys it even before it takes inward roots itself and can truly mean something to those converted in no way voluntarily.

For the zealots of the new faith teach the eternal damnation of the ancestors, and soon grave-robbers dig up the mounds of prehistory with gold-greedy hands. Woman, until then highly revered as close to the divinity, is now considered as in league with the devil. A previously unknown martyr creating cruelty sets in because of this merciless conversion in the north.

It took centuries before the uprooting of the Germanic tribes through the folk wandering and the upheavals of the change of religion entwined with it were halfway overcome. And when Christianity, in the lust for power of its priests sunken to pastors, in the corruption of its relics, threatened to become deformed, it was a Germanic morality that in the reformation saved it from shameful decline, and Germanic blood that with the help of Gustav Adolf's Dalecarlian saved it from the intervention of the Counter-Reformation.

One point with pleasure again and again to alleged or actual shortcomings of Germanic man. He was a drinker, gambler, passionate - when the Romans ruined him for base profit. They practiced blood revenge against the murderer - at an age when frivolous crime was effectively combated.

Germanic vengeance, which usually stood in the service of peeved honor, is gladly and often scolded, but seldom does one blame the Semites for their mercilessly cruel demand: an eye for an eye, a tooth for a tooth. Not with them, no, with Germanic man did the icy air of paganism blow, or its tiger claw show itself, or however the blossoms otherwise fall from the tree of such *"knowledge"*.

But if we try to again base the German on the Germanic from which it stems, then it is characteristic enough that it is always the moral that shines on us as a model, and that this is found nowhere else in this manner.

It is not about writing on runes again, although it could in fact lead us to a straight-growing, German, festive script.

It is also not about enlivening our crafts with Germanic ornamentation, although the results would certainly soon be very important for style certainty and style formation of higher art as well.

It is also not about taking the old, moving heroic sagas and divinity sagas, and not always only the already so often portrayed Biblical and classical material, for a newly blossoming literature and pictorial art or also elevating the eternal values of old Germanic religiosity in artistic shaping.

Finally, it is not merely about giving our children properly grown (wuchsrecht) names.

Rather, completely different values stand before our eyes as guiding:

> The leader and the following:
> Honor, male loyalty,
> Youth associations,
> Germanic law,
> Reverence of ancestors and love for the clan, for the hereditary farmstead,
> Regard for the community - today we call it the social idea
> The sanctify of woman
> The family as germ cell of the folk,
> The homeland, love.

They are not merely ideas, not merely views, rather also institutions. All are blood-bound and timeless. They are valid for every cultural level. We do not need to reach back to them, we merely need to give the validity appropriate for us to the self-evident, from which we were diverted to our detriment. Solely, the grasp of the Germanic essence given to us as well is the decisive thing here.

The Path to Ourselves

Cultural institutions that we have adopted from outside, from the surrounding folks, are to be judged from this inwardly grasped center.

Much that is Indo-Germanic has again flowed to us through these institutions in elevated, refined, even deepened form, admittedly much also altered and alienated. We will not want to dispense with what is appropriate for us, not want to disturb what has developed historically in its genuine effects. But we must ensure with a passionate devotion that what is most native to us gains room to grow from its own, now already long enough hampered energy.

Here it is about acting similarly to among the other racial elements that co-determine or want to co-determine German essence. What proves itself all too alien and wants to destroy us, such as the arrogant influence of Jewry on our German culture, that we reject?

The other, historically, and inwardly bound to German essence, is to be fulfilled from this or overcome. The folkish idea of National Socialism can prescribe nothing else here than the duty to inner truthfulness, responsibility, totality, and provide nothing else than elbowroom for real freedom of conscience in the opening of significant decisions.

Basic questions, which today are being wrestled with everywhere, are native law, native faith, native education, and rearing.

The nine commandments of Aryan law already show the direction.

For faith, important things result from the world-historical and idea- historical view. But the question of how far something Aryan lies based on Christianity is not at debate here and just as little the religious question at all. In this regard, it should be remembered that the National Socialist German Workers Party takes the standpoint of a positive Christianity without tying itself to a specific denomination.

The attempt to infer a fundamental opposition between this position and a championing of the native is not justified. Humanism, too, did not and does not stand in opposition to Christianity, even though it conveyed the eternal values of the pagan antiquity of the Greeks and Romans. So why should it not be permissible that we finally want to know elevated the eternal values of our own antiquity and likewise of the whole northern racial legacy?

One can, if one wants, proceed from the standpoint that the religious denomination must first stand firm before one can think about rearing and education; but one can also proceed from the standpoint that rearing and education must first provide the foundation upon which, from a sufficiently broad view of the world, a worldview can grow that is not threatened by experiences and knowledge, hence also does not need to avoid both, and lays a solid foundation for all outside the dogmatic sphere of the denominations.

In life, one cannot be separated at all from the other, faith from knowledge, affirmation from doctrine. Every nursery has its religious foundation or suffers from it being too scant, and each school aims knowing that it offers a firmness of a faith or suffers from it not really succeeding in it.

Humanism & German Education

Humanism, upon which our higher education rests for centuries, is like such a faith and was, because not bound to dogmas, possible next to Christianity. Its foundation is not Greek or Roman heroism, rather a folkish idea, the idea of the towering worth of two Indo-Germanic folks, of the Greek and of the Roman, of antiquity.

It was a strong and valuable counterweight against the withdrawal from this world, into which precisely inwardly very German human beings not seldom fell because of their Christianity.

It needed the healthy balance in the nurturing of body and soul, and it needed schools with a genuine, very ambitious and completely idealistic goal of education.

Finally, it needed contact with high, and related, cultural goods and the stimulus to increase them.

But in its old form, in can no longer satisfy us. We do not seek the classical man, rather we want the German one.

For us, the Greek has for a long time no longer been an absolute humankind value, the cosmopolitanism into which it lost itself does not mean the fulfilment, rather the loss of its folkish idea, just like Greek democracy was not the fulfilment, rather the loss of the old Greek nobility idea.

The Greeks could not do justice to the Persians, the Romans to Germanic man; what they did not understand, they viewed as barbaric.

Only when they all too narrow field of view of antiquity is burst, do the world-historical background of Indo-Germanic man and the idea - historical achievement of the Nordic race and the worth of old Germanic culture open, which in its outer radiance does not radiate equally only because it is rougher and more reserved; for its inner values are the greater ones.

For us as heirs of these values, Indians, Iranians, and Germanic man also belong to Nordic antiquity. The philology of these folks, along with the corresponding archaeology, can certainly not be all treated in the schools, and already the Greek and Roman have their difficulties. Even more important is the yield of this research as respectively reachable and close to life portraying, formative, will-shaping result.

Aside from that, we demand permeation of the school, even the higher ones and the universities, with German spirit according to portrayal and content so much that antiquity reaches the correct, still guiding interval from us and gives us stimulus and room for the previously denied native foundation for what is most native to us and for a new spiritual shaping, in which all strata of our folk can take part in the interval.

Classical man becomes for us the northern racial one, and the cultures determined by different race are in part prerequisite for his creation, in part they stand at his side. So, humanism and its ideal of education can flow naturally into the folkish and racial idea of National Socialism, and the path is opened to also honor the other Nordic cultures and the foreign-racial determined cultures in their value. The Nordic race and the German folk do not need to be overbearing or even to degrade the other culture-folks as barbarians or incapable of genuine culture.

The result must be that a genuine German education and an energetic rearing paving its way replaces the humanism that has fulfilled its mission in the life of our folk. The results for faith and that religious affirmation can only be blessed.

CHAPTER

4

GERMAN EDUCATION

Two dangers threaten the developing German human being: rearing delusion and education delusion. The educators of the old school believed that all people are equal and education can achieve its goal with everybody. If one encounters difficulties, then one only needs to employ more and better educators and teachers.

Insight into the processes of hereditary and the fatefulness of the genes has destroyed this delusion. There are limits to rearing, even education. They can be broadened under favourable conditions and through suitable means, but not overcome. Much that the individual educator does not achieve can be performed by the educating force of a well-delineated community. If the traits are lacking or if they are too weak, then all effect is ultimately in vain, however.

If the traits are especially valuable and decisively effect in a certain direction, they triumph even if rearing and education have been lacking for long stretches. The young mind seizes at the decisive moment with natural force what is necessary for its thriving and growth and constructs for it its inner and outer life. It triumphs even against an oppressive environment or at least can do it, in the event the outer conditions are not all too unfavourable. But this it not true for the average person; he needs rearing and education, and even the extraordinary talents are endangered without it.

The teachers of the old school believed that it depends on knowledge. Knowledge was supposed to encompass everything worth knowing. And what would not be worth knowing? So the subject burst the school, but one did not take that too seriously. The pupils earned for test and diploma and earned their right to advancement and employment. Certainly, if he wanted to achieve more, he had to sit longer. The ability to devote oneself to a cause, even an intellectual one, was killed in favour of flat practicality considerations. Nobody portrayed the moral damage of this system of justification better than Lagarde.

It is understandable that an education that came about so had to become a pseudo-education and stood open to all decaying influences. Dismantling of the justification system and of the exaggerated claims for a preliminary education for the occupations, which can only be a *"bad training"* (*"Verbildung"*), is the next and very urgent commandment. For there depends on this as well the lowering of the marriage age of the above-average educated young people, who previously married the latest and reproduced below average.

The statements by Lagarde characterized the situation already back then:

- First: We cannot educate in our schools as long as the parents of the children who sit in front of us are not educated.
- The second: The pupil sits in school, gaze fixed on the door and not at the object of instruction.
- The third: One cannot educate, rather only for something.
- In this sense, we add: We want to educate - to be Germans.

One should overestimate education as little as physical exercise. But one should also not underestimate both. The same is true of knowledge. It has educational value only where it has a will-shaping effect and is mastered in the will's direction-shaping. Used in this sense, its educational value is decisive.

Clarifying our desire, our feelings, from knowledge, from concept, crates, as Fichte has determined, character. Every education is character shaping. Character means what is imprinted, what is binding according to orientation. For each, it is the prerequisite for his nationality.

Each German must wrestle for German character, for German unique stamp. He has the raw material, because he is a German. And that means German education. One can have it to a very high degree with little knowledge; and a shocking lack of genuine education can easily be tied too much knowledge.

Education is something that must ripen from the inside toward the knowledge flowing in from outside, must receive a stamp from it, must prove itself on it and from it, yes, even, when necessary, must triumph against this influx.

The relationship of knowledge to education is roughly like stimulus to sensation. If the soul lacks the stimuli or if it is over-stimulated, then it dies.

Measure and selection of the allowed stimuli, educational impulses, are already the first test of character.

Hence, it is not all the same, what knowledge, what subject we consume. Instead, we should nourish the little fire of our disposition with pure woods, so that it grows into a mighty blaze, giving light and warmth.

We need orientation-forming knowledge, and this used so that its value becomes clear for the whole, for the folk - and so that this, too, stands out, just like all genuine knowledge is not dead information, rather expression of living struggle.

Knowing a lot does not make it, rather each must start at the post given him, and it will be shown that it is always a centre from which everything else opens up, if one seriously goes into the depth.

The Educational Value of the Subjects

Each field of science or subject already has its educational value (Bildungswert) in that much must be learned, noted, clarified, before one can build upon the fundamental realizations the higher ones. The order in which this construction takes places and the listening in and looking in at the object at which it is directed simultaneously poses a very essential training value (Erziehungswert).

Each field of science, has the endeavour to comprehend the world totality from its perspective, and not, say, merely from the portion of the world forming its object. Two sciences very diverse in each other may serve as an example: geography and anthropology.

Although geography merely wants to describe the world, it must, in order to do that, stray into the universe; the first pages of the Atlases display this, and every map shows lines whose meaning points above the earth. But it must also delve into everything that exists in and upon the earth, into the history of the earth (geology) and into the living creatures which populate the earth, especially man, the states, the cultures. So it reaches into all sciences, into the natural sciences and the social sciences, and the entire world is reflected in it.

Anthropology is similarly extensive. Its object, man, has conquered the entire world, even intellectually. All knowledge of the world is human knowledge. If one views it so, then nothing does not also belongs to anthropology. Certainly, one will not always go so far and, in order to master the object, also seek limitation.

But thrusts into the whole must occur from each subject. Whoever is really knowledgeable in one area and has not encapsulated himself as an expert also knows how things must go in the others as well. If he even surveys a few subjects lying farther apart from each other, then this can mean much more than a so-called general education.

No course of instruction can be complete, none should be that, and it is already bad, if it is overfilled; for the intellect (Geist) and the orientation (Gesinnung) of the learning person should not become exhausted and uprooted, rather solidified.

Above all, the teacher needs a view of the visible totality of the world and of his own place in both. He must hold himself back from immediately teaching much about it, since it easily has the effect of a *"tendency"*. The self-willed person who matters most rejects it, the ambitious person whom we do not exactly want exploits it. All roads then seem too short, and their end is always viewed as the same.

Instead, the object must be sounded, and the conclusions regarding the whole must result from this alignment. They must be conclusions and not short circuits, steps and not leaps. They must lead to the goal, but the hand must not lead them. Otherwise, instead of the materialistic, liberal, Marxist, Bolshevik, democratic, centrist tendency, we just have another tendency again, whereas the folkish and racial fundamental idea of National Socialism demands truthfulness and clarity.

Biology, Genetics & Racial Hygiene

Biology is fundamental, the science of the driving forces of life, then its branch, genetics, which also offer the laws of life, finally the practical application in racial hygiene.

Biology shows creatures in their worlds. We learn how creatures adapt to their environment, what part of it becomes noticeable to them and how they react, become effective. There results from this the distinction between observed world and working world and the dovetailing of both into the environment.

The concept world receives is meaning from the observing and working creature. With lower life forms, the observed world is often tiny and encompasses just a very few traits. With man, it achieves the highest manifoldness. Through the sciences, it is further broadened and systematically expanded. The technological practical applications of the sciences then also broaden the working world of man and assure him of a certain power over his environment. In that biology unrolls this on the great background of its material encompassing all life forms, its world-view gain is especially great.

It also provides an insight into the process how life, on the highest level of its becoming conscious, can make itself so free that it can dare, with ultimate inner responsibility, to take into its own hand, shaping, a race advancing to such advanced knowledge, in order to assure the escalation of this freedom and the existence and increase of its culture.

The means to achieve this goal are offered by genetics. The genes are fate, but the laws according to which they pass down to open the prospect to guide this fate. One can clearly separate the deformed, especially in severe cases, from the well-formed, and even if one knows little about the initial causes of the deformity, the consequences of its spread through heredity are all the better known. This is joined by the determinations about the frequency of bad genes and their effects. The valuation of the cases of above-average success and its heredity likewise remains realistic.

Finally, life itself displays achievement and confirmation. It is to be ensured that the highly valuable reproduce above-average, and the clearly deformed not at all. Racial hygiene then explains and bases the individual measures; its application leads to population policy.

New moral values result. If in the old moral doctrine the individual was of infinite value, whom one, however, in practice often treated badly, now the value of the individual is determined, agreeing in theory and practice, from considerations that are aimed at the folk whole and the culture whole.

The old medicine aimed at preserving and tending individual life, the new one, beyond that, also has an eye on coming generations and hence must not hesitate to limit the individual existence to itself in case it cannot take responsibility for its reproducing.

It affects all areas of life: mate selection, marriage counselling, inheritance law, criminal law, voting right, welfare, health care, physical exercise and much more.

Human Science, Race Science & Folk Science

The object of human science (anthropology) is initially the human body and the diversity of its forms among present-day and earlier folks of the earth.

It reaches, beyond the concept population and folk, to relatively constant, even if not *"pure"*, races, from whose mixture it aims to deduce, according to the laws of heredity and with regard for environmental influences, the physical traits of the folk tribes still close to the beginning primal races, then individual folks (Einzelvölker), folks (Völker) and populations (Bevölkerungen).

Its material leads in part farther back into primeval time than the oldest remains of human activity, and it also leads to where human creatures rose from the animal to above the animal. Although it could not provide final clarity here, basically everything fundamental has been clarified, namely the origin of man and his relationship to the animals. His origin steps into the light of natural science, and this simultaneously also provides the natural historical foundations for humankind's history of ideas, his races and folks.

We see how diverse the races and folks are, physically and mentally, all according to their natural tendencies. From these natural tendencies then result the structure of the cultures as self-portrayal of their bearers.

Cultures are always driven forward and escalated only by individuals, by individual talented human beings, and by individual folks and races. Others must take up the new culture-deed and pass it along.

Among the races and folks, finally, the location of one's own nationality determines. Culture-geography, science-geography, world commerce and even world trade: what are they, if not attachment and expansion to this science!

Prehistory, World History, Culture & Science

What folk science portrays primarily in space, - world history shows mainly according to time.

Not everything that has ever occurred is significant world-historically. To write world history means to evaluate. But evaluating does not mean proceeding arbitrarily. Many people say: science should not evaluate! But one can also say: who should do it, if not it?

The value of achievements, inventions, institutions shows itself in how they prove themselves, thus over time, in history. But where a value is found, an unworthiness (Unwert) is rejected, a will stands behind it, which stirs within us.

History hence has a will-forming effect, repelling and attracting, character-forming, like hardly anything else. It is the College of politics.

Our world-historical field of vision has broadened. The ancient history of the oldest cultures, Indo-Germanic man's fateful path, German prehistory, the continued effect of these mighty processes into the present and into the questions moving it, is more complete and clear than ever before.

It is about solidifying this intellectual possession. If people do not know where they come from, then they also do not know where they should go. They are like sailors without compass and stars on a stormy, dark night sea.

A special area of world history is general culture science (allgemeine Kulturkunde), and it simultaneously plays into folk science, while history in the narrower sense is more political history. One will know too little about Germandom, if one does not know its place in the building of human science and folk science and its stride through world history and its accomplishments - measured by pictures that a general culture science can depict.

The goal must not be sunning ourselves in what we have achieved, rather we must measure ourselves by what others as well have become great in. Two individual areas especially come under consideration in the process: religion and law.

Comparative theology shows us the religious struggle of the folks, the abysses of the souls that open up, but also their creative energies. The great religions become comprehensible from their early stages and prerequisites and enter their idea-historical connections.

Another branch of culture and science, jurisprudence, affects not only valid law, rather the shaping of law overall. Beyond Roman law, we see the German one native to us. We seek its sources in Germanic and Aryan law. But we can adopt only the essential core, the psychological orientation (gesinnungsmäßige Einstellung); individual institutions only as an exception and sensibly altered: the totally different cultural level of today separates us from the special stamp of that time.

Folk Science & Language

Such considerations already lead very close to folk science (Volkskunde).

That folk science branches off from German cultural history and the science of folks rests on that wherever leading social strata have produced high cultures based on lower strata, the folk custom of the lower strata wants to be treated separately.

Folk science finds out the survival of old customs and traditions and builds many important bridges to our own prehistory. So it supplements homeland science. Previously, it paid too little attention to differentiate in this tradition between native and alien and to put the native in its Germanic and Indo-Germanic, northern racial context. It is urgently necessary to catch up with that here.

Each should know about the totality of his nationality and not live merely in the culture of an upper stratum. He should also know the saga and fair-tale, folk song, dance, children's game, practices and customs of folkish tradition. Within it, native, old nature is contained in a plentitude and clarity from which we can often deduce more and more that is close to nature, more joyful, more future-mighty than from many creations of high art and literature. Educating oneself from this property gives genuine folk-closeness and homeland bond.

An important application of folk results are festivals when one tries to enliven them with old, meaningful custom. Dusty relics remain misunderstood; and it can only hurt to heartlessly put them on display. But if the dispositions, unnoticed and yet penetratingly, are prepared for the old and its inner worth, which must happen with understanding and from a distance, then even apparently already dead values can become truly alive again - like, say, a dried out seed, that sown still strikes roots.

Admittedly, folk science cannot overcome the difference of the strata, but folk property gives energy for new folkish deed, quite similar to the traditions of the German and Germanic past standing on an older cultural level.

There is only one more area where a similarly large treasure of German nature lies hidden: the German language. It likewise has something arranging, direction-giving, obligating within it.

Speak proper German! If you take that seriously, it penetrates into all your thoughts and shapes you anew from the inside out: this produces a self-stamp, preserves character.

The demand for proper language also leads beyond the German to the tribe-related languages. Should one say *"better than"* (*"besser als"*) or *"better than"* (*"besser wie"*). Here, it is not the word usage of preferred poets of authors that can decide, rather in all Indo-Germanic languages there is a different word for the positive than for the comparative. Departure from this comparative word would be a further loss of the Indo-Germanic manner of speech in German.

The demand for proper language is an excellent test for the will. Whoever takes it lightly or brusquely pushes it aside will seldom take anything else seriously.

The same is true for the demand for language purity, to avoid dispensable foreign words, for the wrestling with the simplest, most understandable, most suitable expression.

Finally, one should pay attention to German name-giving, even with proper names. If they are ancient, then one should see that one understands them. Relationship results from proper names that reach back to the spiritual property of the Edda and the rest of old Nordic legacy.

Society, Science & State

Now one should remember that culture, law, practice, custom, language are all just expressions of social life, in which nationality is at work.

Certainly, today we are surrounded by a social life that could make one despair. If one did not know that, we will soon fill it with a new spirit. We are already beginning with the festivals.

The old social doctrine with its colourless general concept of human society was not at all aimed at answering the question about the essence and nature of a German society as folk community, at showing us what is a historical coincidence in these institutions, how it could also be different, and making our judgement free and the yardstick and pillar of a new desire.

The old economic doctrine remains even more distant from the goal. One treats the manifestations of economic life as iron necessities resulting from concepts that would have to be valid even for Mars.

That it could be about the economy of the German folk, one left totally out of the game. And yet, it is so clear: here a land that is delineated, economic-geographical tolerably, or actually intolerably, and here a population in which the consciousness and desire of its nationality blare up again and again, giving direction.

Finally, the state as well is not an end rather only means to an end. It must not fossilize, must remain open to motion and serve the folk. Behind the state idea and above it, there arises the Reich idea. Reich is more than state and timeless, inner goal of the whole folk.

The land, the folk, its history, they are the prerequisites for the national economy. The land places demand on the folk and summons its unique nature, but the Nordic race still always present in this folk despite all fateful events, the German within it, again forces it under its power, fertilizes it with its blood, moistens it with its sweat, shapes it according to its high, direction-giving will.

Mathematics & Physics

Not yet named are the sciences of inanimate nature, physics with its branches, then mathematics, then philosophy, finally the whole extensive area of technology, that means the practical application of the various sciences from medicine to technology and in the narrower sense to politics.

That happened with intention, even if with each of these subjects with a different one. Not all areas of thought, research and knowledge overall are supposed to be discussed here, rather, it should be found out how they lead to German education.

Many of the just named sciences, so it seems, would without major changes in their content also have to be represented in a French, Russian, English, American, Japanese education. Mathematics and logic are valid universally, the laws of nature are universal and necessary.

The direction in which these realizations are sought and found is time-determined, location-determined, blood-determined. Logic and mathematics were already discovered in everything essential by the Greeks, but not any other folks still again. Even among Europe's racially closely related folks, differences in mathematical talent show themselves.

Newton and Leibnitz, the Englishman and the German, in the service of similar research tasks, escalate synthetic observation in mathematics into calculus. Descartes develops analytic geometry and Galois group theory, which in its application to the fundamental principle of algebra, likewise lies toward analytical thought.

A special manner to escalate the formalistic in mathematics, even in its application to the physical, seems to characterize Jewish thought. A perfect example is Einstein's ever more subtle reality theory, which, where it has previously shown itself, merely shows a seductive manner of observation, but has not yet grasped any new physical facts. However, we do not need a game with the formal, rather contact with reality.

The emergence and history of the sciences of inanimate nature as well lead to the folkish and racial idea.

In Babylon, astrology sets in a caricature of a science of the stars, but simply not yet astronomy, the genuine science of them.

Egypt, China, Mexico as well do not create any natural science on their own.

But when the Greeks' knowledge of natural science sank with the exhaustion of their race, the Germanic folks, opening up the world through folk wandering, Viking voyages, crusades, exploration expeditions, also take up the old voyages of discovery into the realm of world knowledge.

Viking spirit continues in nature research, heroic devotion to the object and to truth, urgently searching for the moving causes.

It means a fateful departure from this orientation, if a new *"modem"* direction in physics awards leadership to mathematics, which is only a make-shift means through which one assures oneself that the object has been completely thought through, instead of to the reality lying at the base of research, which must be traced to laws.

The great nature researchers are oriented toward knowledge, not ingenious play, also not acquisition. They are all primarily northern racial human beings. The history of the natural sciences, the life of the great nature researchers, gives testimony to the spirit of the Nordic race.

Philosophy

Philosophy can become more essential than everything else, if it gives itself the goal of native thought. By native kind, the Nordic one determined by race and nationality is meant. Admittedly, previously, this orientation was as good as totally lacking.

What circulates as philosophy has very diverse worth. We have little reason to be inwardly deeply satisfied even with the course of the Greek and then with our own German philosophy, even though the great thinkers tower over everybody else and, through the intrepidity of their intellect and the strength of their character, have been the truest educators.

Greek philosophy soon collapsed from its original height with the exhaustion of the Greek folk spirit, and the German one took up all too much of the legacies of this decline and was always severely retarded. One paid homage to an abstract thought and hence sought neither the conditions of native thought nor did one pay attention to its sources.

The fundamental orientation was individualistic or universalistic; one saw the distress of the individual or of humankind; one seldom saw the distress of the folk.

The excess of unnecessary foreign terms in the affected professional jargon, the wind-bagging with empty concepts, makes most philosophical works disagreeable, and the outsider finds it difficult to distinguish between appearance and genuine content.

Hence philosophy, as it exists, contains many dangers, especially for an inexperienced, youthful spirit, which is unrealistic, formalistic thought only all too easily draws under its power. It can almost more easily have a false educating than an educating effect, if care is not taken for the depth. But it was a great German philosopher who coined the expression of the revaluation of all values. We now prepare to carry it out. A wealth of experience and a will aimed at an inner law that goes beyond all experience must take part in this work. Many sciences strive to flow into the future's mentally clarified view of the world and to decisively influence it, because they have brought to light new important results and because a spiritual arrangement of the old with the new is necessary.

Greek philosophy developed under the leadership of mathematics and the exact sciences. The beginning that biology and history just barely took among the Greeks no longer succeeded, for the creative energy of the Greeks had been paralyzed as the result of race-mixing. Similarly, the beginnings of German philosophy, bursting the chains of scholastics, stand under the sign of mathematics and the exact sciences. But the influx of biology, the science of living beings, and of history, prehistory, primeval history, cultural history, the science of folks, folk science, race science, genetics, happens among us with much more thorough preparation, likewise at a distance and so that the discussion of this rich property only now for the first time comes due in a large framework.

All our philosophers would have had to philosophize totally differently if they had known what we know today. The thinkers of the German future will complete the action of the new sciences coming together into a new view of the world and have to adjust these results against the old view of the world. There will be no lack of fertilizing minor and major crises, and a final state of knowledge, a lazy hide upon which one could lie down to rest, will and can and should not be tanned. One cannot cheaply expect to reap high values from philosophy if one does not already bring something oneself. It is part of the ever escalating misery of the time that one was again and again ready to spin seepage of every kind from philosophy into literature to the point of game playing, which would not have been possible at all, if they had been faced with real knowledge and yardsticks. To possess these simultaneously means being capable of judgment.

Technology

Aside from ability for judgment, we need ability for performance. All sciences have their technological application in one form or another. Applied science is technology.

We never forget that the technician, in the broadest and best sense of the word, is a world conqueror, that the Nordic blood in his veins perhaps pulsates the strongest, and that all science that gets at the existence of the world essence-researching owes its glory to the leadership of this Nordic spirit.

The most pronounced representatives of these fields, in the event their talent is so strong that they have little room left for the others, may safely be a dreamless "educated"; in exchange, they engage all the more decisively as formative men, shaping their time, intervening in the fate and thought of their folk.

But we may also ask of them they see their relationship to the whole of this folk not merely in the basic features, rather that they have also let this knowledge and look at themselves have a thorough effect, that they have taken it seriously, themselves act accordingly and bring others to act accordingly.

Philology, cultural history, art have been overestimated in our folk for centuries in an all too external manner. Now one is perhaps indined to again underestimate them and science overall. Instead, we must finally find the right balance. The applied branches live from the theoretical ones and perish if they decay. Conversely, theory experiences its true fulfilment because it is applied. Only both sides of culture, the self-reflective one and the one leading to action, produce the totality of life.

Certainly, it is necessary that the does not merely apply, rather purposefully apply. The drive for reputation and gain can set such goals, and a genuine idealism in the service of a higher goal can set them. Selfishness and materialism degrade technology, action for something higher ennobles it.

The machine is an example. One has drivelled much about its demonism. But the machine is dead iron, and beyond that, only what man makes out of it. It can unburden people and free them for higher goals, and it can crush men and make them unemployed, according to how one uses it. Inventions only turn against their inventors if they fail in the decisive thing.

But our hopes for technology are very strong and aimed at the right thinking in its application. Also, the concept of technology broads quite a lot for us, since now not merely the sciences of inanimate nature produce technological applications, rather also the science of animate nature and the historical sciences now push toward cultural technology, toward the new medicine, toward population policy and cultural policy. Just that this part of technology is first in the process of development. But it will prove itself as at least equally decisive as the earlier.

Medicine is a technology, if, broadened into racial hygiene, with utilization of the exiting insights and knowledge, it is employed to heal the folk body, and, broadened into cultural policy, to heal the folk spirit, so that the German folk succeeds in what the other northern racial folks previously failed: to reach the goal.

Cultural technology, cultural policy has not merely a formative effect, where the whole people knowingly absorb them and their goal, rather they also have a re-forming, re-shaping effect. The landscape is re-shaped through roads, trains, bridges and much more, the economy through machines, rationalization, etc.; but that is merely environment. It goes much deeper, if the folk itself undertakes to reshape itself and in such a way that in the process new, higher formation becomes possible and the racial properties of the higher order to benefit the racial properties of the first order instead of working against them.

That is not progress that on its own guarantees the course of the world or an absolute intellect, also not a loyal look up at a beckoning infinity next door, rather the hard demand of self-assertion. Standing still already means failure and is the beginning of the end.

Art

Similar to technology, art as well is an escalated ability, similar as with technology, with art as well. From the beginning on, this ability stands under an inner direction above the merely technical. This inner life alone matters, its wealth and its power to speak to us from the work.

The formative power of all art rests on this, both the purely decorative, which Germanic man has brought to the highest perfection, and illustrative art, in which the Greeks were for a long time rightly our model, as well as literature, the theatre and music, all three of which reach back to Indo-Germanic root.

The art of the folks of Nordic race differentiates itself so greatly from the art of the other folks as the respective culture and all their spiritual products. Art can never be separated from them. The artists always stand in the middle of the life of their folk, carried by it and escalating it into the blossom of their art.

Art history under the leadership of the folkish and racial idea has not yet been written. It would have to bring a similar re-evaluation as world history on a racial basis, for which merely the beginnings exist.

But art history is also not the only, also hardly the best path to art. Works of art were created so that they can speak to us themselves. Admittedly, they are blood-determined, folk-determined, time-determined and have, the more they stem from high cultures, also the more manifold prerequisites. But the higher a work of art stands, the closer it gets to the ultimate, the eternal, the more these prerequisites recede behind its inner content, and the more compellingly it can communicate itself.

What says it? Seldom something that can be reduced to concepts. Quite the opposite, the conceptual is easily a great enemy of the artistic.

One also hardly reaches the core if one characterizes the beautiful as its goal. At least, one must view the concept as beautiful for us anew. There is much northern racial art that is not beautiful in the sense of antiquity. Instead, it communicates an inner bearing, and this most movingly, if this bearing is simultaneously life experience, and a final judgment and affirmation. And also lies then the native or the deviation from it.

Hence, the artist cannot merely be an illustrator, rather is always also an educator, and art forms and educates at the same time. It can point the way to new ideals, a new life bearing.

The state of art is similarly a test for the worth of a culture, of a nationality, like the state of the sciences or the employment of technology. But while the sciences are even more difficult to access, the farther they progress in their results, because with them one builds on the other, art can, yes, must, again and again start anew, and the duty of truthfulness is at work within it in such an elevated, and despite all severity simultaneously mitigated form, that art is all the more easily accessible, the more it succeeds to express transfiguring the innermost essence in the simplest manner.

The Whole Goal

In closing, let it be warned against wanting to absorb from all these areas, subjects, curriculums something, or worse, everything; the result would be that nothing could be saved of the whole, which is what matters. An over-filled, over-stimulated stomach cannot digest. Better to do a little seriously than do nothing properly.

However, we need the complete picture of German education in order to select accordingly for the respective special education purpose, and in order to apply what is selected according to this whole picture. The important impulses of educational and formative value will emanate from such teachers who are totally rooted in their subject and have developed character in the ultimate spiritual-moral sense and can show their pupils what it comprises, and can put demands to them. Education that is merely possessed is too little; it must also influence the service of the folk whole. It is a task for each individual according to the gift and limitations given upon him, but it is also a task for the whole, for the folk and the genuine folk state. Above all, the education system has distributed in the folk the legacy of the folk, its racial properties of the higher order, and to ensure the passing along, so that the survival and increase of the culture is ensured.

The dangers of excessive foreign influence, frequency and misdirection must be met by the educational system as well, and since through education it forms the ideals of the culture-bearers, it is also owed a very significant share in the awakening of the correct and necessary yearnings and energies of the soul and the preservation of the culture.

To expel the foreign, to expand the native, preconditions deep-reaching education. Likewise, the determination of the essential is a task of the power of judgment schooled through education. Only both together create the preconditions that the environment will shape as needed so that the culture-bearing racial properties of the first order remain preserved and become solidified.

The educated person, in the sense of German education, must not, as the educated person previously was all too often, be an uprooted person. Rather, the roots of his education must reach back so far that he has found his way back into his inner homeland, which emanated from the north, has presented itself in the creations of the Indo-Germanic folks, from sacred legacy remains at work in the German folk as the blood heir of Germanic man and now again strikes roots in the German homeland, in the German home, and should ripen toward a new future. It is unnecessary that everybody knows all that expressly, yes, for the majority is hardly desirable. But everything that he knows should be applied directly or indirectly according to this outline, so that at any moment, as much of it can become alive as this moment demands.

The goal is set so high and so extensive that it obligates long-term. And we affirm this obligation long-term: first in the schools, then in life, and so generation after generation.

The situation today is completely different that even recently. The old nationalism has fed too long on the intellectual property of unforgettable, farsighted leaders like Arndt, Jahn, Lagarde, and has fossilized.

But now new forces are stirring in our movement. The new nationalism has idea again, and it offers resistance to all the storms of the present, and it has a socialist heart.

We want unconditionally the new German future. For us, it

should not be a poor imitation of some died off past, not a helpless and feeble repetition of what once existed. Rather, we want to absorb within us all the energy of the past and process and re-shape it within us, so that this future becomes. It should not be a rebirth of Germanic antiquity, not a Renaissance, rather a new birth of German essence in mind and limbs.

CHAPTER

5

KNOWLEDGE, FAITH & DESIRE

Knowledge

One can differentiate: the knowledge about race and folk, and the knowledge that the race, the folk, has gained over the course of its existence. The first group of knowledge encompasses race science, genetics, folk science in the broadest sense of the word; the second group of a very independent section of it, in which the structure of all available sciences is contained.

This knowledge provides certainty within the boundaries drawn for it. It provides confidence; it obligates. Also, solidifies the faith in the German future and in the desire aimed at it. It alone secures for this desire, the action promising its success. One often hears said: knowledge divides, faith unites. But that is a false conception and comparison, which aims at a deficient, splintering knowledge alienated from its foundation, while we mean the total, right one. All genuine knowledge has its foundation in faith and a unifying force, which no other one will achieve so soon.

Good will and a heart in the right place must be present, but they alone do not suffice. Even a firm hand can only take a good hold, where straightforward gaze has first seen what is necessary. Knowledge is the eye, the will, the hand.

Without insight, even the best will is blind, without will, even the most correct knowledge paralyzed. Just that if the blind man carries the paralyzed man, the paralyzed man shows the blind man the way, both reach the goal.

But like every comparison, this one as well is imperfect; for the will gains eyes for itself and knowledge gives it legs.

It is correct that the race makes it, that the blood does it; but it does not do it through an imagined, effortless legacy memory, rather through its moral and spiritual force. Even all inspiration rests on it and on the sense for reality and the supra-reality (das Überwirkliche) that governs in it and within us, and only becomes due if much serious inner work has prepared it. It is also correct that knowledge gives power. All technology proves it. But it is just as correct that our knowledge and are power are very limited. There is no cause for arrogance.

We agree with Newton, who recognized that he had merely found a few shells and mussels on the edge of the ocean of the unfathomable, and with Kant, who stated that the observations and calculations of the astronomers, aside from many admirable things that they taught us, have shown us as the most important thing that the abyss of our ignorance is so great that human reason cannot imagine it at all without this realization.

Even the laws of genetics, even race science, even the world-historical experiences with the previous cultures, even the entire structure of the sciences overall mean very little, if one considers how incomparably more we do not know.

This our knowledge exists, and much heart's blood sticks on it. This knowledge is too little, but, by human measure, it suffices for the purposes that now matter. What may still lack must be added by our faith purified by it. We can bum neither this knowledge nor this faith out of our minds and hearts. We can never let ourselves be talked out of the duty to act according to both and our best conscience.

Science

The might of the racial and folkish idea is so great that even science cannot escape it. The more clearly we see that science itself is best race result, the more determined we are to drive science farther toward the previous race thinking and to employ it in a time of the folk's greatest distress for the securing of its existence and of its future.

Science and research have their *"biological function"* in the folk's life. With their knowledge, they broaden its perceived world, arrange it, clarify it and make it possible to take it in at a glance; with the technological practical applications of this knowledge, they enlarge its world of effect, permeate it and make it governable. In order to remember how science broadens the perceived world, one should think about the world of the large, which the telescope, and the world of the small, which the microscope, opened up; and in order to understand how science broadened the world of effect, one should think about mining, ship travel, the airplane and how depths, expanses and heights previously inconceivable to us become accessible and useful in their results. Science, the pure and the applied, as well as history, as well as population policy, performs a service to the folk. In order to perform this, it must be free. That means it must attentively and conscientiously follow its most own law: truth.

Science that one commands what it must prove, or which one forbids what it has recognized, or one prescribes where it has no business and where it must search, so that it does not become uncomfortable, is not science. For its fundamental service lies precisely where, through thrust into fresh territory and through new insights, it corrects outdated views and champions them against the prosecution by those who care more for their dogmas than for the truth. The opposition hence exists not between science and faith, rather between science and fossilized piety, such as the bitter struggle of the churches against science, and over it with the goal of bringing it into dependency, has proven again and again.

As important as it is that science preserves its freedom, only a quite general rule lies. To fill the framework that is proved by it, that is the actual task.

Value of the objects of research and the knowledge it can yield, however, is not to be determined by materialistically according to use. The leading researcher is not guided by the user, neither his own nor any other, which might result from the desired scientific knowledge, rather solely the passionate will to find out how *"it"* is. The selection of this *"it"*, his object, given pronounced talent, is as little voluntary for him as for the artist. Even the researcher is closely bound to his object, and the significant one to the significant object.

Whether the research leads farther, whether it promises new insights and prospects, or at least completions and clarifications of existing results, that matters. There are countless areas in which one also researches, countless truths which one can also find out, and which are not worthwhile and are neither suited to really enrich our knowledge nor increase our productivity. One just must not judge such questions by appearance, rather with consideration and prudence. Often, an important basic insight has arisen from the examination of apparently secondary things. Often, very theoretical observation has yielded fateful practical applications. There is much petty, visually deviant, fruitless activity. It is to be turned off.

Even individual questions are to be taken up from the whole of science and solved toward this whole. If the energy of research is not dissipated on the secondary and if it is employed for important objects which promise the fruits of new knowledge, then the practical applications cannot remain lacking; but to base upon them in advance would be the death of any genuine research and also silly. For if the gaze is directed at the use, it does not cling firmly enough to the object which initially matters solely. Also, before one has the knowledge, one can hardly correctly estimate the value that it may bring, and this is the most difficult with knowledge owed to new, creative inspiration.

All truth is bound to object, the finding of truth is race-bound, science has been created almost only by the Nordic race.

The Jewish non-spirit (Ungeist), the object-bound, which has diverted from reality-near research into the formal and merely conceptual-constructive, is to be purged.

A new spirit must grip the scholars and researchers from the new thinking and the new orientation of will.

Important research tasks were neglected, because the folk alien current of the time, hostile to the German nationality, opposed them. In the social sciences, German prehistory is an example, which brings us knowledge about our ancestors and the oldest relationships of the Nordic race, another is the study of Iran, which opens new looks at Jewry, Christianity and knighthood from the side of Aryan essence and must clarify our folkish idea.

The action of science in the folk's service can take another step in technology. It lies in technology that either it must set itself tasks or that they are set for it.

The distress of the folk sets such tasks. That means at the same time that one must aim at the important and reject the superficial. An ongoing effect, even on research, will emanate from that.

Finally, science must more than previously find the path to the folk. If it presents its knowledge in understandable language free of foreign words, that will already be a big help. But it must create it, already for itself as well, from inner tie to folkish thought as simple as possible.

It must not please itself with a handed down reputation, rather it must always achieve its reputation anew through the inner value of what it offers.

Faith

The National Socialist worldview rests with its basic idea of folk and race not merely on knowledge, rather a strong faith also dwells within it. Both and the newness of this closed spiritual and moral action have as a result that many raise objection after objection precisely out of considerations of their faith, which draws from other preconditions not yet balanced against our own.

One accuses race science of being a crude materialism, drawing only from the appearance of the body and not respecting the energies of the spirit and of the soul.

No misunderstanding can be greater. For body and soul are a union for race science, behind which stands a nature that sets the basis for both. The psychological and behavioral characteristics are part of race, just like the bodily one.

Materialism teaches that the soul is a perspiration of the body, spiritualism that the body an incrustation of the soul; the doctrine of the body-soul (Leibseele), toward which race science leans, is visibly equally distant from both doctrines.

One further accuses race science of breeding racial arrogance and judging folk comrades according to their racial traits and not according to their moral personality.

That, too, is a misunderstanding. Not the racial traits, rather the performance decides. The racial traits enter the overall assessment of the folk comrade only as a partial consideration, and only with the weight due to them in view of the folk whole.

If we posit a new ideal of beauty and value according to inner bearing, then this, for example, in mate selection, but also in all other selection, without which it never has been and never will be possible, has no other result than any other ideal as well: namely that those who correspond less to the ideal must be pushed into the background. Only it is without a doubt more moral and more just, if in mate selection the genes are more important than the moneybag; and it has completely different consequences for the folk whole, if the beauty of the leading race is important instead of that of another one. Seen from the folk whole, the new ideal lies toward its preservation and increase.

One accuses racial hygiene of infringing on a person's right to one's own body through limiting deformed offspring.

It is strange that people who occasionally value the body champion. This sanctity of the body is precisely very little.

Until a few decades ago, one had no reservations against castrating the genetically healthy choirboys of the choir in the Sistine Chapel in order to let their voices, artificially kept high, proclaim God's honour; but now it is supposed to be despicable, if folks threatened by the generic feeblemindedness, criminality and mental diseases, exclude from procreation such misshapen people, where their reason still suffices, for their own comfort and, besides that, for the blessing of the coming generations.

Finally, one says the idea of taking care of the whole folk according to new knowledge would mean that we presume to intervene into creation, to play creator ourselves - a titanic endeavour, which must be followed by divine punishment.

Yes, many already evoke our punishment.

Again, nothing but misunderstanding! If it is rightly a service, if the individual disciplines himself, rations his hereditary factors and balances them against each other and possible, and where they are weak, improves them through exercise and schooling, and if it is rightly a reproach, if he neglects that, although he could, then the same must be true for a folk.

Nobody may oppose the folk and deny it what one demands from the individual human being; nobody may decry the folk as godless, if it does what one decries as godless with the individual human being, if he neglects it.

The knowledge that we apply stems from the blood of our race and the legacy of our folk, and if the term *"God given"* is supposed to have a meaning at all, then it certainly has it here. It would be sinful if we were to please ourselves by bragging in this gift or to disrespect it as worthless and wanted to not use it over the one or the other. It is a pledge of higher mercy given upon us, and our duty follows from this.

Whoever closes himself to it, or even resists it being fulfilled, has either not yet understood what is at stake and not yet grasped that it is now about thinking, as one previously thought in individual fates, beyond these individual fates, to think in fates of folks and act accordingly or in his blindness he does not want at all that our fate, upon which his own also depends turns.

Desire

So the final decision lies in the desire.

Opposing will must be won. We bring so much that admonishes to reflection that we trust the winning force of this property. But we cannot wait all too long for it to succeed against unreasonable obstacles. For the commandment of the hour, which must not pass unused, is at our heels, and decisive, life-essential things tolerate no postponement.

What we bring is not compulsion, rather freedom.

The question of how moral actions are possible occupies us much less than the task to create space for them based on measures that a new morality puts into our hands, in which the old one fulfils itself on a higher plain.

The question as well as whether human will is free moves us much less than presenting to German man his inner law and his world historical responsibility as guideline for his will.

The sign under which we fight symbolizes a controlled force that expands ever farther from the inside. It is an ancient sacred sign of salvation that has accompanied the fateful path of the folks of the Nordic race.

Salvation means *"whole"*, heal means *"make whole"*. But it would mean more that the repair of the broken, of the damaged, and also more than the healing of a wound by the mysterious, total energy of the living. For this force can do much more. It can produce from the seed a very fresh, rejuvenated and, if we start correctly, ennobled life, for which fresh energies and possibilities grow. This ever-expanding force within us and its controlled employment, that is our path, the path of our blood, of our spirit and of our confirmation (Bewährung) through the healing deed.

CHAPTER

6

GERMAN CULTURE & LITERATURE

Dr. Hans Friedrich Blunck Honorary President of the Reich Chamber of Literature, Member of the Reich Culture Senate and of the Senate of the Academy of Literature

At first glance it may seem strange that a poet and writer of fairy-tales has been chosen to write this article on German culture policy, when so wide a choice from among leading politicians was available. Perhaps, however, the selection was symbolic, because creative artists in Germany to-day are concerning themselves, as never before, with the rising and falling fortunes of their fellow-countrymen. Certainly that romantic age which consigned the writer to an isolated garret existence has gone for ever. If only in this respect, we, in Germany, have turned from the romantic period of Europe to the classic, when some of the great creative thinkers were also leading personalities in the State.

Another motive made me particularly happy to accept the invitation to co-operate in the writing of this book. I was born in Schleswig-Holstein, a country jealous of its Anglo-Saxon heritage, where we are all intensely aware of our relationships and where also, since the time of Storm and Kroger, we have been fully alive to the dual nature of the creative artist's work. This duality, so frequently found in England, is probably a common inheritance.

Galsworthy, who was my friend during the last year of his life, always seemed to me to be the perfect example of a well-balanced individual, who possessed at the same time the attributes of a strong leader. He was an Anglo. Saxon of the type that we, in this Hanseatic land, appreciate and love – not only from personal sympathy, but also for old sake's sake.

Occasionally I discussed with Galsworthy the part that writers could play in our restless Europe, and I still remember the tolerant smile with which he said that we writers would never be able to act and write as statesmen, because our ideals, conceptions and convictions must always be bound by some inward necessity. Perhaps, he said, our position may be, for this reason, particularly strong, and perhaps it may not be a bad thing for the people of our respective countries if, by using our imaginations, we can cover with some sort of nobility even the coldness and self-seeking prevailing in European politics.

In considering Germany's present culture policy, a starting-point must not be made at the complacent and satisfied Europe which was commonly shown to the British and French reading publics before the German revolution. Instead, we must examine those terrible times through which our country passed, when it seemed impossible that it could ever rise again from defeat and hopelessness, especially the latter. A military collapse can never produce such bad effects as an injustice; the broken promise that lay between the Armistice and the Peace Treaty was probably that which most deeply hurt the feelings of our humanitarian population, and indeed still does. For long it seemed that all attempts to build up a new Reich were condemned to failure, and as if a death dance had begun which would end in the complete ruin of our thousand-year-old State. Let it not be forgotten that the Communists were on the point of securing the largest representation in the Reichstag and that all the restraints of the old order were breaking down. The middle classes, supporting a liberalism which they did not understand, and pervaded with the instinct of self-seeking and self-preservation, were apparently no longer in a position to offer any resistance. The currency, after one breakdown, was threatened with yet another collapse. Thousands of peasants were driven from their homesteads, which thus became the property of the mortgagees, and the workers – sick of unfulfilled promises – were definitely hostile to the bourgeoisie. Hundreds of pretentious developments in the sphere of the arts were hailed for a moment as substitutes for religion, only to disappear a few weeks later. Words and figures were bandied about, only to sink again into obscurity, like spooks which had strayed for a moment from the land of shadows. A small gang of alien immigrants from the east drew their profit from the sorrows of a whole nation, spreading like a blight over the country. The cradles stood empty, and everyone lived for the hour or the day because there seemed to be no future. Whatever sensibility or pride remained was destroyed by humiliations suffered through our foreign policy.

These were the conditions out of which National Socialism arose, and beneath its wing our *"Wartburg Circle,"* literature's adventure against the forces of decay, was formed. The *"Academy"* remained firmly a left-wing institution, while the powers of progressive conservatism collected around Johst, Beumelburg, Münchhausen, Kolbenheyer, Grimm, Schäfer, and Vesper (the author of this article is, of course also a member of this group). The glowing poetry of certain younger men, amongst thern Anacker, Schumann, Böhme, Möller, Nierentz, Eggers Meusel, Brockmeier, Oppenberg and Helke formed an accompaniment to the political development of the times. Amongst the dramatists, I would specially mention Rehberg, Bethge, and Langenbeck.

There is no doubt that these groups were the first to awaken a response in the minds of the common people throughout the country. Post-war artistic achievement had no wide appeal, based, as it was, either on eroticism, or concerned with expressionism or cubism, and directed only towards a small public. The right-wing opposition, however, succeeded in winning the appreciation of the youth. Readers, turning away in disgust from the eternal psycho-analytical studies, found a young art flourishing in their midst, that reminded them of their national history, that made their country-side bloom again and whose subject matter was not limited to descriptions of city life. Here were poems, tales and essays for which the man in the street, almost unknown to himself, had a secret longing. In short, the rift between writers and people, that had yawned wider and wider during the post-war years, started to close again. Here was a literature which – though not ignoring the old forms – was rooted in the countryside, was closely in touch with the feelings of the people but was also vitally connected with the political happenings which were then heralding a new era.

The culture policy of the State has shown clearly enough that the debt of gratitude to creative artists has not been forgotten.

Perhaps it should first be made clear what is meant by this expression *"culture policy,"* for misunderstandings arise only too easily in the babel of modern Europe.

It is the duty of the State to cultivate harmony between the political and private life of the people – neither more nor less. Therefore, without limiting, or acting against, the achievements of the individual, it seeks to promote the broad conception of *"People's Culture,"* to encourage their inherent taste for decoration, for picturesque celebration and for their own ancient customs, and to direct these so that they conform to those *"Christian ethics"* which are valid throughout Europe. The German State also accepts it as a duty to discover those who are capable of speaking for the people, and who, every now and then, have tried to gain the light of day, only to be overshadowed by the acceptance, formerly so readily accorded, of foreign values. Those who wish to know something of this subject should read the book, The Tyranny of Greece over Germany, published by the Cambridge University Press. German history can reveal over and over again how the so-called educated classes kept their distance from the mass of the people, and attempted to form their own autocracy. The present Government, on the other hand, seeks to emphasise the connection between the old literature and the new, and the relationship of both to the people. This is not achieved by laying a compulsion of any sort upon the creative worker. The Government does reserve to itself, however, certain rights of choice and the right to issue recommendations. What other more fortunate nations accept as a matter of course, namely the possession of an art inherently national had still to grow up in Germany and to be assiduously cultivated.

This problem was solved in 1933 with comparative ease, largely thanks to the opposition of the *"intellectuals"* to the former regime, an opposition that had sprung up before the revolution.

Thanks are also due to the energetic preparation of the ground and to the intellectual values which the modern conceptions *"Nationalism"* and *"Socialism"* had been given in Germany since the pre-classic, the Sturm und Drang period, and since the time of Herder and the youthful Goethe.

Nothing, surely, could make a stronger appeal to the artist's sense of justice than Herder's conception of *"Nationalism"* – that is to say, the ordering of Europe in accordance with the self-governing rights of the nations, and the refusal to recognise any interference on the part of neighbouring States. I am well aware that the word *"Nationalism"* has a different meaning in every European country, and it is one of the Continent's greatest misfortunes that this apparently universal expression creates nothing but misunderstanding and that we all mean something different when we use it. Nationalism in England means more or less the same as *"Imperialism"*; in France it means *"Chauvinism"*, while in Germany it means exactly the opposite, namely, the right of all nations, in the sense of Volkstümer, to develop along their own lines, within their borders. In Germany, in fact, it means nothing but an aspect of the old longing for freedom, the dream of a Europe in which the free nations live peacefully as neighbours.

Again, the religious sensibilities of the artist cannot be more profoundly stirred than by the conception of true Socialism, as the fittest expression of national solidarity. The rationalist, or Marxist, foundation of Socialism was overthrown because it was based on class warfare, but it was a Socialism grounded in religion that attained power in Germany with the arrival of National Socialism. I must go further: I must maintain that it did not only attain power, but it gave Europe the most perfect example of living Socialism extant, so far, of course, as this could be achieved by a people which disposed of no raw materials. It is hardly a matter for surprise that the artist, who ever inclines towards the essentials of faith and pity, eagerly embraced the theories of the new State, that he accepted Nationalism as self-government of the people, Socialism on religious grounds, and that at the same time he rejoiced exceedingly over the new and intimate relationship with all his countrymen, without the barrier of class prejudice that was the gift to him of the new State. I will not conceal that it was the younger writers of the new movement who passionately accepted the change, which was a difficult matter for those who had fought hard and long in the ranks of the opposition, and upon whose individualistic ideas the demands of the time placed hardships, which forced them for a space into loneliness. It may seem paradoxical, but I am quite sure that the new leaders of Germany are fully aware of the essential loneliness of the creative artist. All the same, however, German writers to-day know what happiness it means to stand before a crowded, youthful audience on a winter evening and to read to them ballads, stories or essays that meet with true appreciation. The writer who stands up and reads his works to a crowd of factory workers, and who sees the meaning of his words truly understood by them, realises enough to want to hold firmly to the relationship between writer and people, which seemed at one time to have been utterly lost.

Perhaps I have dwelt too long on the consideration of that background against which the astonishing change in Germany took place. I thought it necessary because so many of my English friends interest themselves in various details of the organisation of the Third Reich, but know little of the intellectual *"behind the scenes"* of the change; I might jestingly say that we, the third – or continental – Anglo-Saxon group, feel that we have a certain responsibility towards the Reich on behalf of our next of kin in the United Kingdom, and that we would so gladly restore the bridge that existed for five centuries between England and Germany, so perhaps my discursiveness may be pardoned. In compensation, I will answer more pointedly the questions – What were the practical measures taken in connection with culture policy in new Germany? and How was the close relationship between the State, the people and the artists – desired by National Socialism – achieved? For (and of this there can be no doubt) the relationship exists, even though the voice of complaint is now and again raised, and even though there are aspects of the achievement that could be improved. These things are unavoidable when sweeping changes take place. On the other hand, there is no organised opposition group, a fact that has led our neighbours (who cannot believe that it is really lacking) to suppose that it does indeed exist, but has been artificially suppressed. My friends, anyone who knows anything about the soul of a writer and about the courage of the creative worker, must surely also know that a real opposition cannot be suppressed, and must realise that the wonder of the German unity is that it is actually based upon true community of heart.

This miracle of which I speak is the more remarkable in that the economic situation of the artist was anything but rosy – as is probably always the case in times of revolution and change – during the first few months of the new regime. Adherence to it was, therefore, a sacrifice rather than an exploitation. It must be admitted at once that the State very soon took steps to ameliorate the initial difficulties, but such emergency assistance is not to the taste of the artist, who wishes to live by his work. Nevertheless, financial assistance given to artists during the first two years of National Socialism amounted to more than had been available for two decades before – a sign of how seriously the situation was taken. It was not long before the new theatre replaced the old organisation destroyed by the revolution, and before Kulturgemeinden (Culture Communities) were created which, even in the smallest German towns, invited writers to deliver lectures and readings, and made them the principal speakers at country gatherings. At the earliest possible moment attempts were made, through the organisation Kraft durch Freude (Strength through Joy), to bring to the ordinary workers their past and present heritage in literature, music and art. From the moment that National Socialism achieved power, it strove to make of the *"proletarian"* the *"fellow-countryman,"* equal heir with all to Germany's intellectual kingdom. In 1936, no fewer than two million workers visited exhibitions and attended plays, and often lectures, organised in the factory buildings. Two literary *"agencies"* were set up, and helped in their own way: endless patience was expended in the reading of manuscripts, and it was recently announced that all the writings *"hidden away in Germany's old chests and cupboards"* had now been examined as to their literary merit. Everything of value was handed to one or another of the great publishers, but in future it will be the task of the latter alone to make their selections.

Among the great organisations in modern Germany, there is scarcely one that has not concerned itself, either more or less, with the arts: they all possess literary departments. Successes have not everywhere been equal, but this was hardly to be expected during a period of four years of drastic change. However, good will has nowhere been lost, and we must realise that when we see excellent cheap reproductions of the classics and the best of the moderns being eagerly read in peasants' houses, in the labour camps and in the barracks; our public buildings decorated by the work of living sculptors, and finally, the love of music being cultivated in villages as well as in city concert halls, then we must also see that work of much value is being done, which outbalances the occasional failures. This revolution, that outwardly forced political aims and social necessity so much into the foreground, and that found so many bitter words to utter against the *"anti-social influence"* of the arts, has, in spite of everything, greatly profited from the teachings of history. It is fully aware that artistic achievements alone are able to justify to posterity a change in the form of government. This new Government, composed as it is of members half of whom are men who originally intended to devote themselves to some creative work, knows, because of its inward religious convictions, the importance of artists as mediators. This government, rooted in opposition against rationalism, is well aware of the nameless longings of the people it governs, of their dreams that sway between heaven and earth, which can be explained and expressed only by the artist.

Perhaps more important than anything else that has been mentioned so far is the legislative attitude of the State towards the sphere of the arts. The position of the arts in the State was defined by the Chamber of Culture Law of October 1933, which represents something entirely new in Europe.

Probably the clearest description that I can give of this law is that it has given practical shape to the establishment of an artist's guild or corporation.

The principle of the Corporate State, which has been applied to some of the changes made in Germany, has, for many decades past, been expressed in political writings. Other countries than Germany have concerned themselves with this idea: Literary Congresses in various countries have constantly urged that the relationship between the arts and the State should be defined, British and French delegates having been particularly insistent on this. No better solution has, however, as yet been found than to demand an unlimited *"liberalism"*- whilst the corporate suggestion was consistently rejected.

The newer governments have sought another way out by reviving the idea of autonomic *"Companies of Artists"* such as existed in medieval times. The Chamber of Culture raises the groups of artists from the ranks of the people, and makes them self-governing. The duty of self-observation is also laid upon them. For the present the State has withdrawn various privileges, a withdrawal which certain individuals regard as limiting, and which they describe as *"bureaucracy."* These privileges have been replaced by a Corporate Constitution, providing for several sub-Chambers, each of which is entrusted with the task of ordering the professional relations between its members and of assuming responsibility for their professional affairs. Each is invested with full legislative power. It should be mentioned that the activities of the Chamber are limited to German nationals, and that artists of foreign extraction are directed to set up their own organisations.

Altogether there are seven such sub-Chambers, those of Music, the Plastic Arts, Literature, Wireless, Press, Theatre and Cinematograph. They are united under the control of a central authority, whose decisions are binding upon all. A Reich minister stands at the head of the Chamber, and the individual sub-Chambers are mostly under the presidency of creative workers. For instance, the architect, Herr Hönig, was at the head of the Chamber of Plastic Arts and Richard Strauss was the former president of the Chamber of Music, which is now under the leadership of Peter Raabe. For two years I was privileged to be President of the Chamber of Literature, and I was succeeded by Hanns Johst, the famous dramatist and lyricist. Another writer, Rainer Schlösser, is at the head of the Theatre Chamber, but the Radio and Press are managed by experts in each subject, rather than by artists.

The decrees made by the Press Chamber have received more attention than those received by any other. There has been approval as well as disapproval. The latter is doubtless caused by certain hardships that are bound to be the result of any revolution: nevertheless we have through these prevented our revolution from assuming the proportions of the one in Spain, and I am convinced, however much the duress may irk the individual artist, that, even in this, we have pursued the right path. The great change in the press that has so served to stimulate and refresh us, is what I might call the" publicity" of subscribers and editors, which has completely swept away the influence formerly exerted by anonymous contributors of money, by certain economic circles and by interested denominational groups. The reconstruction is proceeding apace, and is based on the principle of the personal responsibility of the newspaper proprietor and his editors. Anyone acquainted with our press as it was towards the end of the parliamentary democracy must be well aware to what a degrading dependence upon industrial concerns it had sunk, and how many cliques – preserving touch with our foreign enemies – attempted to influence home policy in order to serve their private ends. All who lived through those times realise to-day how sane an effect the application of the principle of personal responsibility for word and deed has had.

I have nothing to hide or to extenuate, and I am perfectly aware that, at the inception of the revolution and for a short period afterwards, it was impossible to express a free opinion. This has rapidly changed. So long as attacks are not made on the State itself, and so long as nothing is published that could lead to a disturbance of the public peace, there is no ban placed upon the free expression of opinion. Do not let us always return to times that lie behind us, but when did the makers of any revolution permit any opposition propaganda to be published? Let us rather compare soberly the question of dependence and independence as it works out in Europe to-day, and, if we do so, we must admit that in the majority of countries around Germany (I forbear to mention names) where the press is still in the pay of economic groups and political parties, the freedom and security of an editor are far more severely restricted than in Germany. I think that in this respect (as in many others) the fact is not sufficiently appreciated abroad that a strong opposition is lacking not because it is suppressed in Germany, but because the conviction of opposition is also lacking.

The number of newspapers sold, which decreased between 1933 and 1934, has once more gone up, so that in many cases the original sale of the papers has been greatly increased. The attitude of the general reading public is most clearly indicated by their demand for those publications known to be free from any suspicion of outside influence, i.e., periodicals, magazines, etc. In 1935, their sales figures increased by 9%. as compared with 1934, and a further increase of 15%. is estimated to have taken place in 1936. These figures apply in connection with about 1,500 important magazines and periodicals. The Press Chamber, like the Chamber of Literature, dispenses a considerable relief fund, which expended over two million marks in 1934, and the same sum in 1936. An Act that came into force in April 1938 provides pension schemes for all editors of newspapers.

The Chamber of Music, apart from giving great support to the cultivation of music throughout the country, has issued regulations governing the fees paid to musicians. The International Congress for the Protection of Authors' Rights, which recently met at Berlin, confirmed the fact that Germany had found the surest and quickest way of dealing with this distracting task. If we should now approach our neighbours with a legislative suggestion to make authors' rights more secure internationally, we should do this not so as to snatch at a leading position for ourselves, but simply because, so far, we have in this respect gone further than any other country. What is probably the greatest proof of this statement is that unemployment amongst our German musicians, which amounted in 1934 to 50 %., is to-day insignificant. Every British visitor to Berlin, Munich or Hamburg knows that the repertoire of operas has been enlarged and that our opera houses are often *"sold out"* long before the dates of the performances, whilst – in 1932 – our actors and actresses frequently played before empty or half-empty houses.

The most difficult position in those earlier days was doubtless that occupied by the Chamber of Plastic Arts. The bourgeoisie that, perhaps without much taste, took pleasure in supporting the efforts of sculptors and painters, withdrew the greater part of its custom in this respect after the economic crisis of 1929, which led not only to the unemployment of the artisan, but also to that of the artist. The new Government felt itself compelled to set an example, and very soon no public building was planned without an artist having a share in its design.

The State has erected many buildings in the past few years, but the position is still very difficult. The new stratum which is to give private orders and commissions to the artist is forming very slowly. During the year 1935, the Chamber of Plastic Arts, apart from large sums expended on travelling, provided 800 old and young artists with holidays varying between fourteen days and four weeks in length. Further sums, reaching a very high total, were also spent in giving relief to artists who had fallen into poverty, and the Chamber instituted, or provided the stimulus for, between three and four hundred competitions offering valuable chances and prizes. The chief work in this connection is the provision of new facilities for exhibition and the training of a new class of would-be purchasers, a task which has met with very considerable success during the past couple of years. Europe's finest exhibition building, the Haus der Deutschen Kunst, at Munich, was inaugurated by the Führer himself in 1937.

The Chamber for Wireless reports that the number of listeners increased from about 4,000,000 to 7,500,000 within the space of four years. I do not know whether this increase corresponds to those recorded in other countries. But I do know, from what I heard when I paid visits abroad, that the German programmes are popular outside the borders of the Reich, especially those broadcast by the Deutschlandsender and the short-wave transmitter, which are designed to keep our countrymen abroad in touch with the mother country. There is little to say regarding the activities of the Cinematograph Chamber, under the first-rate managership of Professor Lehnich: the international prizes awarded to German films are sufficient witness of their effectiveness. The number of people who go to the cinemas has increased by 10% per annum since 1935.

The Chamber of Culture Law has probably been most effective in the domain of the Theatre and in that of literature. The theatres, which after 1928 grew emptier and ernptier, and which could attract a public only by producing the most sensational plays, were not in 1933 instantly able to win back their audiences. The continuous appeals of the new Government to the theatre-going public to encourage the arts, and the influence exerted by the theatre-goers' organisations (which, for the first time, included the workers) little by little produced a change.

The visitor to Berlin to-day is frequently surprised to find that all 40 theatres of the capital are playing to full houses, and that the theatre is actually in the midst of a great boom. The number of State or municipally owned theatres mounted from 155 to 178 between 1933 and 1936, and the number of people employed in theatres increased from 20,000 to 26,000. State subsidies to the theatre amounted to 12,000,000 marks a year, and were principally placed at the disposal of theatres with ancient traditions, which had fallen on evil days, but which nevertheless remained fully conscious of their local or classical importance. I have not space here to relate anything about the new plays that have been performed, or about the open-air theatre or the people's theatre, which can accommodate up to about 5,000 persons. It would be better to hear an expert in these subjects, and still better if English people would make a trip through Germany and see for themselves what is being done.

Under the Chamber of Literature are organised not only writers, but also booksellers and libraries and everything that has to do with the production and distribution of books. When the Chamber of Culture Law was passed, the book trade had an ancient organisation of its own, and there was also an Authors' Society of little importance, which concerned itself solely with financial matters, and which was becoming more and more an institution of the great cities alone. It is putting the situation in a nutshell when it is said that the movement of 1933 was nothing more nor less than a rising of the regional instinct against the exaggerated centralisation in the capital. It is certainly true that literature very plainly revealed that its support was for the healthy movement, rooted and grounded in the people and the country, against the circles of eastern emigrants and undesirable groups in the capital. In spite of the unrest of the times, a strong impetus has been given again to regional forces in literature.

Economic protection remains, of course, an important part of the Chamber's work. The advisory bureau on legal matters has been re-established, and disputes between publishers and authors mostly yield to arbitration, both parties being members of the same Chamber.. Subsidies from the State, and privately offered contributions, make it possible to give assistance in cases of real distress, through the instrumentality of the Chamber.

All these, however, are means that were employed before, and they do not suffice for the work of the present Chamber. Soon after it came into existence and was provided with full power under the Chamber of Culture Law, it started to fight for the new rights of the arts. It has opened its own book trade school, at which hundreds of young people not only learn to know the literature of the Middle Ages, the Classical period and the Romantic movement, but learn also to form their own opinions regarding our present-day literature by discussing it with their fellows. Not only this, it has caused the 10,000 lending libraries of Germany, some of which catered for a very inferior taste, to increase their stock by about 33%., in which they had to include the classics and some at least of the best modern writings selected from the literatures of all nations. The Chamber of Literature was also able in 1935 to offer a number of prizes, which were the result of private subscriptions and which represented a value of about 2,000,000 marks.

One of its best ideas has proved to be that Book Week, organised each autumn, in which everyone is asked to examine his books and to buy whatever he can afford to improve his library. Book-buying, which had markedly suffered, has, since 1934, increased each year by about 15%. This is a large increase when it is considered that political books, which were heavily bought during the pre-revolutionary years, monthly lose in popularity, and that book-buyers are found more and more amongst the youth of the country, who are eager purchasers of the omnibus collections published by the Insel-Verlag, the Diederichs-Verlag and the Müller-Verlag.

The passing of the Chamber of Culture Law was followed up by the formation of a Reich Senate authorised to deal with Germany's cultural problems. It is composed of the presidents of the various sub-Chambers and a number of the foremost young writers and artists. From amongst these, experts are chosen to see that the new law is properly applied, and from them the State seeks to forge the instrument by which the intellectual leadership of the people may be made to march side by side with the political.

This is the position after four years of ceaseless, breathless action. We know, of course, that changes which give specific rights to the company of artists, the effect of which can hardly be appreciated as yet, need a decade or two in which to develop. We are pleased that, during these vital years, we have laid the foundations for the new order. We know that we have made a great many mistakes, but it is surely better to achieve something, even if mistakes happen, than to sit with folded hands awaiting the fate that seems to threaten the whole Continent.

Germany's revolution is not yet over: the smoothing of the paths, the rounding off, is just beginning. We know that every revolution produces a number of restless spirits who have to sow, as it were, their wild oats before they can adjust themselves to the new order of things. Our task is not over: it has only just begun. But we are pursuing a road that daily becomes clearer. We are in the midst of a time which is characterised by a will, surely everywhere perceptible, to create juster principles of religious brotherhood and freedom amongst the nations, a Weltanschauung by which the arts are no longer regarded as belonging exclusively to the intellectuals, but as instruments in the hands of an all-pervading Power that guides our human destinies. I have often spoken about these things with my friends abroad, many of whom still seem to think that the writer should be lying in the sun when he is not puzzling his brains at his desk. How in the world, they say, can you, for instance, who have just read us your poems and fairy- tales, possibly occupy yourself with matters of State? What have they to do with you?

I have already told of Galsworthy, who felt differently about this, and who devoted a great part of his life and his writings to the service of his people. I believe that we, the peoples inhabiting countries whose shores are washed by the North Sea, hold similar views on these matters, and that we also understand the dual task which has been laid upon our shoulders. And if people go further, and ask me whether I approve the restraint that is used and the *"Prussianising"* of the arts, then I, poor innocent, merely shake my head over the wisdom to be found in this world. Does anyone really believe that we, with our solid peasant stock and honest bourgeoisie, would permit restraints to be placed upon us that we did not voluntarily accept as a means to bridge over the difficulties of the moment? Does anyone believe that we – who, after many a hard struggle, have just regained our national unity – would be content with the policy pursued by the new Reich if, in our hearts, we disapproved of it? Does anyone think that we artists are so unemotional and passionless that we would calmly tolerate circumstances we were unable to support with all our belief-belief in a better world and a new fulfilment of our God-ordained task?

We will not utter reproaches, though it is often a bitter thing to be misunderstood. We want nothing but to build up our own State without external interference, and in the way we think best both for our people and for the young art that is flourishing with us now. May people learn to leave us alone, if they cannot understand us, because we have no designs on them and only desire to complete in peace the great work we have undertaken. But where we find sincere friendship we return it with friendship, and we only ask our friends to be patient for a little while, if they cannot comprehend everything that happens in the Reich. Our people, since 1918, have been compelled to bear almost unendurable burdens – is it then surprising that they are longing for a newer and juster world? We have won through to inward and are now awaiting outward peace and justice. We artists are probably the most strongly desirous of peace, because we are building the new homes of the four arts, and believe we are building them well.

Does this sound arrogant? I do not think so. We should learn to be more tolerant not only of the old, but also of the young. It should be realised that the spirit permeating our continent is one that has many aspects, and that it is variously expressed in every nation. Let us also always remember that the nations are not really so far apart from each other as jealousy and unrest would have them believe, and let us hope that the feeling of European solidarity, which our thousand-year-old history has taught us to appreciate and in the development of which we Germans would like to take our share, may once more be awakened. We artists of the Reich are teaching this creed to the children of our people. But we still miss the outside response.

CHAPTER

7

WOMEN IN THE
NEW GERMANY

Frau Gertrud Scholtz-Klink Reich Women's
Leader

When National Socialism became the ruling power in Germany
(1933), we women realized that it was our duty to contribute our
share to the Leader's reconstruction programme side by side with
men. We did not say much about it, but started to work at once. Our

first concern was to help all those mothers who had suffered great hardships during the War and the post-war period and all those other women who - as mothers - have now to adjust themselves to the demands of the new age.

Acting in accordance with the recognition of these facts, we first created the Reich Mothers' Service (Reichsmütterdienst), the functions of which are set forth in Article I of the regulations governing it:

> The training of mothers is animated by the spirit of national solidarity and by the conviction that they can be of very great service to the nation and the State. The object of such training is to develop the physical and intellectual efficiency of mothers, to make them appreciate the great duties incumbent upon them, to instruct them in the upbringing and education of their children, and to qualify them for their domestic and economic tasks.

In order to provide such training, several courses of instruction have been drawn up, each of which deals with one particular subject only, e.g., infant care, general hygiene, sick nursing at home, children's education, cooking, sewing, etc. These courses are fixtures in all towns with a population exceeding 50,000, whilst itinerant teachers conduct similar ones in the smaller towns and in the country. Every German woman over 18 can join them, irrespective of her religious, political or other views.

The maximum number of members has been limited to 25 for each course, because the instruction given does not consist of theoretical lectures, but takes the form of practical teaching to working groups, where questions will be asked and answered. Since the establishment of the Reichsmütterdienst, i.e., between April 1st, 1934, and October 1st, 1937, some 1,179,000 married and unmarried women have been thus instructed in 56,400 courses, conducted by over 3,000 teachers of whom about 1,200 are employed full-time, whilst the remaining 2,300 (also possessing the necessary qualifications) act in an honorary capacity or in that of part-time instructresses.

Our next concern was with those millions of German women who, day after day, attend to their heavy duties in factories. We look upon it as most important to make them realise that they, too, are the representatives of their nation. They, too, must take pride in their work and must be able to say:

> *"I have a useful duty to fulfil; and the work I do is an essential part of the work performed by the whole nation."*

With this end in view, we have created the Women's Section of the German Labour Front (Frauenamt der Deutschen Arbeitsfront), which has now a membership of over 8,000,000. Foreign critics have frequently stated that German women have no chance of earning their livelihood by working in industrial or other undertakings. I therefore take this opportunity of emphasising that more than 11,500,000 women are employed in the various professions and occupations; the Women's Section of the German Labour Front attending to their interests.

Moreover, we are of the opinion that a woman will always find it possible to secure paid employment provided that she is strong enough to do the work demanded of her. This applies to women workers of all categories, irrespective of whether the work is of the physical or intellectual kind. It is therefore the business of the Frauenamt to ensure that women are not employed in any capacity that might prove detrimental to their womanhood and to give them all the protection to which they are specifically entitled. In order to translate these ideas into practice, the Frauenamt has proceeded to appoint a *"social industrial woman worker"* (soziale Betriebsarbeiterin) for every undertaking in which a considerable number of women are employed.

The functions to be exercised by these Betriebsarbeiterinnen are of a general and a special kind. They have to see to it that all women employed in the same undertaking look upon their own interests as identical with those of the latter and that a proper spirit of comradeship grows up among them. They are assisted in their task by the works' leader and the confidential council, and they are in a position to gain the confidence of the other women workers because all of them are comrades of one another.

They have to prevent strife, jealousy, and irresponsible talk from poisoning the social atmosphere of the works, to help those of their fellow-workers who may be oppressed by domestic worries, and to assist in rendering the conditions of work as dignified as possible. To that end, they have to furnish the works' leader with suggestions for any measures that may be required to adapt the processes of work - in conformity with the technical peculiarities of the undertaking - to the natural capacities of women. Finally, they have to assist in the transfer of women workers to other places of employment, in the task of making the aspect of the working premises as pleasing as possible, etc.

This enumeration of their functions shows that they must not only be experienced social workers, but must also be familiar with the actual work. For this latter reason, they are required to devote several months to such work before they are appointed to the post of social workers. During that time they receive the same wages as the other women workers and are subject to the same regulations as they. Similar arrangements, although on a more modest scale, are made in connection with smaller works, i.e., those where the number of women workers is less than 200.

Special care is devoted by our organisation to married women workers with children and to those expecting to be confined. In this domain of social work we provide assistance, in conjunction with the National Socialist Welfare Organisation (N.S. Volkswohlfahrt), exceeding the standards set by the existing legislation. Such supplementary assistance consists in money, food, linen, etc.

I must not omit to add a few words in reference to the women students who spend part of their holidays for the benefit of those women workers - notably those who have large families - who are in need of a week's relaxation in addition to their regular holidays. The students generously attend to the factory work of these women during their absence; and as they demand no wages, the workers suffer no pecuniary loss whatever. In many instances, free quarters are provided for the students by the National Socialist Women's Organisation (N.S. Frauenschaft), whilst the Welfare Organisation grants special facilities to the women on holiday, such as additional food parcels, board and lodging in one of their mothers' hostels and so on. During the first few years of the operation of the scheme, the students relieved the workers to the extent of 57,700 days' work. Large numbers of letters are received by us every day, in which workers and students alike tell us how grateful they are for their unforgettable experience. Works' leaders, too, continually inform us of the beneficial results achieved.

After completing the inauguration of the above schemes, we continued our work in a different direction, i.e., by organising ourselves. We have now co-ordinated the previously existing women's associations and thus created the German Women's Association (Deutsches Frauenwerk), which is sub-divided into sections along the lines laid down by the N.S. Frauenschaft.

The Deutsches Frauenwerk consists, apart from the Mothers' Service already mentioned, of the following sections : National and domestic economy; cultural and educational matters; assistance, and a foreign section. In addition, there are four large administrative departments, viz., general administration; finances; organisation and staff; the Press and propaganda matters, which latter also deals with the radio, films, and exhibitions.

In the section for national and domestic economy, women and girls are trained to apply the principles of national solidarity. They are taught that, in every household, the mother is responsible for the health of the whole family by providing good food and by generally exercising her duties with skill and efficiency.

The cultural and educational section makes the nation's cultural assets available to women; women artists are assisted in their work, and particular attention is paid to the achievements of women in the realm of science. The assistance section deals with the work done by female nurses, the Red Cross, and the air defence society.

The foreign section establishes contact with women's associations abroad, supplies information to foreigners, exchanges experiences with foreign organisations, makes arrangements for seeing the institutions in connection with the work of the Deutsches Frauenwerk, etc.

All these groups are under the general direction of the N.S. Frauenschaft, which may therefore be regarded as the leading organisation, whilst the Deutsches Frauenwerk and the Frauenamt der Deutschen Arbeitsfront constitute the joint foundation for the work done by women throughout the country.

Foreigners have repeatedly asked me about the kind of compulsion exercised to make women take part in all this work. I wish to assure inquirers that we know of no compulsion whatever. Those who want to join us, must do so absolutely voluntarily; and I can only say that all of them are joyfully devoted to their work.

Let me conclude by quoting a remark which I made on the occasion of the Women's Congress held at the time of the Nuremberg party rally (1935):

> *"All the work done by us as a matter of course, which is now so comprehensive that we cannot anylonger describe it in detail, is only a means to an end. It is the expression of the determination of German women to assist in solving the great problems of our age. A spirit of comradeship animates all of us; and our devotion to our nation guides all our efforts."*